This Part Is Silent

A LIFE BETWEEN CULTURES

SJ Kim

W. W. NORTON & COMPANY
Independent and Employee-Owned

In this work, the author recalls various events as she experienced them. The work is not meant to be an exact retelling, but instead reflects the author's memory and the essence of her personal experience.

For information about permission to reproduce selections from this book, write to Permissions, W. W. Norton & Company, Inc., 500 Fifth Avenue, New York, NY 10110

For information about special discounts for bulk purchases, please contact W. W. Norton Special Sales at specialsales@wwnorton.com or 800-233-4830

Manufacturing by Lake Book Manufacturing
Book design by Chris Welch
Production manager: Louise Mattarelliano

ISBN: 978-1-324-06476-3

W. W. Norton & Company, Inc.
500 Fifth Avenue, New York, N.Y. 10110
www.wwnorton.com

W. W. Norton & Company Ltd.
15 Carlisle Street, London W1D 3BS

1 2 3 4 5 6 7 8 9 0

어머니에게 아버지에게

They take from you your tongue. They take from you
the choral hymn. But you say not for long not for
always. Not forever. You wait. You know how. You
know how to wait. Inside 마음 fire alight enflame.

—THERESA HAK KYUNG CHA

CONTENTS

정

This Part Is Silent

ㅓ ㅣ 야 ㅏ ㅣ 야 ? [Dedication]

I wrote this for us. I apologize for the mistakes.

엄마 없는 집에

엄마 없는 집에
엄마소리가 난다
개단위에 숨을 멈춘
난 눈을 감고
더 자고 싶다
다시 일어나면
또 이 소리가 들리겠지
달그락
달그락

부엌엔
잠옷차림에 설거지하는
우리 아빠
아빠 맨손엔
뿌연 밥그릇 하나
진주처럼 빛난다

나무아미타불 관세음보살
[Forgive Me My Eyeballs]

You have cleared out your airy office in Bloomsbury, your exceptional office with the view of dreams, overlooking a leafy square. Before you, the office belonged to a professor, not a professor in the casual American way, a full professor in the British tradition. The professor's retirement meant there was room to hire a new member of staff at the lowest level; you weren't necessarily meant to inherit the professor's incredibly spacious office. For four years, you worked in the uncertainty of his departure, four years as the most junior academic among the non-precarious faculty of your department. You counted yourself lucky to be safe, the last full-time permanent lecturer to take up post before the onset of a hiring freeze. You still feel you were, lucky, for the most part.

Some months before you joined, possibly while you were filling out application forms, the bookshelves were taken down from the walls, as the foundation was crumbling. Over four years you accumulated stacks of books in the space anyway, along with oddities, such as a salt lamp from your students.

The salt lamp is shaped and weighted like a bowling ball. It teeters you as you maneuver into an open seat on the train, the first leg of your commute home. Your students didn't even know that the novel you started as an MA student yourself, the novel that got you your first agent, the novel you couldn't finish on the job, the novel you're not sure you'll ever finish, had been called *SALT*. You actually have very little idea why your students got you a salt lamp, exactly, but it is pink and can fill a small room with a warm glow and you love it and you must remember to turn it on frequently at home, just as you did in your office, so that the salt doesn't melt. Your novel has been melting away from you for some time now. Your novel is about ice cream, ghosts, and race relations, you would sometimes singsong the words "race relations" with jazz hands, and in it, a little Black boy is found dead in a salt barrel. You thought the strange detail was conjured by you, but during your Ph.D. you traced it back to Komunyakaa and grew unsettled that you were undoing his work.

Lena, Lois? I feel her
Strain not to see me.
Lines are now etched
At the corners of her thin,
Pale mouth. Does she know
I know her grandfather
Rode a white horse
Through Poplas Quarters
Searching for black women,
How he killed Indians
& stole land with bribes
& fake deeds?

Once, there was a not overtly racist but rather explicitly homophobic teacher who tried to instill in you that everything in life would forevermore trace back to Gilgamesh. You haven't thought about Gilgamesh nearly as much as you've thought about how much of your literary education was shaped by women who held in their hearts wealth, Jesus & the Lost Cause; for you, it's *Neon Vernacular*.

Komunyakaa writes in "Salt,"

What the children of housekeepers
& handymen knew was enough
To stop biological clocks,
& its hard now not to walk over
& mention how her grandmother
Killed her idiot son
& salted him down
In a wooden barrel.

For four years, you tried to teach your students: What you do matters. Hold yourself accountable; protect your work, keep yourself safe. You tried your best, even if you could barely model such ideas yourself. You are shifting the weight of the salt lamp and your books and feel so overburdened, it takes a moment to register that the person in the seat next to you is asking you something.

This is not the first time you encounter a girl alone and crying in a public place. This is the first time it strikes you that she must be just about half your age. She is asking if she is on the right train; she isn't.

You shift through your books to offer her a pack of tissues. She starts, then, stares down at your extended hand; she begins to cry harder and embraces you, resting her head where your heart is.

You feel yourself flinch and hope she doesn't notice. It has been no more than a handful of days since you stopped wearing a mask on public transport; you forgot once, then it was easy to keep forgetting. The discomfort of the pandemic is constant, masked or unmasked. The unease of eyes on you, the sense of sickening others—you have been navigating such violences for most of your life.

You flinched because your body forgot the weight of a stranger's wholehearted trust. There are things you think you will never forget, things that feel formative at the time of learning, but you do—you forget kindness all the time.

She holds on to you as you get off at the next stop. She doesn't want to call anyone. She is certain she just wants to go home. You move through the crowds together to find the line that can take her home. You move slowly because you both need to. You wonder why these things happen on days you happen to be toting bags of books and a bowling ball of salt. You have to shift her away to stand in front of you on the escalator; she keeps looking back to make sure it's you and you're still there.

You get on the right train and find two empty seats. You catch your breath and remember to hold her back as you reiterate important questions.

Are you hurt?

Do you need medical attention?

Would you like to tell me what happened?

Is there someone you can talk to waiting for you at home?

You believe her when she says no. You believe her when she says yes. You accept that you know only what she tells you. You accept that your fear of not knowing is not needed here. You refuse to let your fear take the space she needs from you. You note the stops for her, counting down to hers. You hold her close and measure out your questions with further refrains:

You have nothing to apologize for.

You are safe now.

You will be home soon.

You wish there was more of you to enclose around her; you wish you could extend yourself to be an airy, warmly lit room. The thought is fleeting, as it must be; it holds as you exit onto the platform with her and walk her to the turnstiles; it holds, barely, as she looks right into your eyes, then, releases you, passing beyond the barrier, looking back just once before merging with the crowd.

A friend from home is visiting the city and invites you for oysters and caviar. Home, in this context, is the nation of America. The city is London, and you have been an academic here for less than a year. In some ways, you know this friend well; in other ways, you do not; you have thought of them often. They say they found your university profile, and you are touched. You are about to say so, to thank them for looking you up.

There's something I've always wanted to tell you, they say.

I often feel guilty when I think about you. You told me once about the work you do, and I didn't get it. I should have guessed what happened to you.

They take your silence to mean that you don't remember and/or that you don't understand. They start to speak louder over your silence.

Those calls you took from women? Staying up all night? I get it now that women do that kind of work because it happened to them, too. I know that now, but I didn't then. I was just a kid.

I wish I had asked you about it, back then. I want you to know I'm ready now to hear what happened.

Everything tastes of salt.

You feel you may be salt.

You have read the story about the woman who

about that man.

You go home and edit your university profile.

The work is not about finding resolution. You try to teach this in terms of writing.

You thought the endless nights of listening for your phone until sunrise had etched into you an understanding. Most shifts, you didn't get a single call. You can count on one hand—exactly, still— the number of times you met survivors of rape and domestic violence face-to-face. When you did, you typically waited with them for family, friends, and those more qualified. You spent most of your time waiting. To best serve, your training taught you to know your limits, to set boundaries and to respect them in turn. You learned to draw strength from the not-knowing. But it is hard, momentarily unbearable, to watch her pass through the barrier on her own.

You can't sleep, seeing her look back at you. You sort through old papers from your now-old office and come across a folder of research for one of your first big events in post, a discussion entitled Reading Bad Men.

At the luminous white heart of MeToo, news of Avital Ronell's sexual harassment of her grad student was breaking. In "I Worked With Avital Ronell. I Believe Her Accuser," Andrea Long Chu writes of academia, "A culture of critics in name only, where genuine criticism is undertaken at the risk of ostracism, marginalization, retribution—this is where abuses like Avital's grow like moss, or mold."

Chu writes, "You can talk about structural issues all you want, so long as you don't use examples of people we know."

Upon investigation, NYU found that Professor Ronell did sexually harass her grad student.

Chu writes:

> Of course power is messy. But there is no complexity in studying forests if you can't recognize a tree from a few feet away. This is not wisdom; it is an eye complaint.

> Structural problems are problems because real people hurt people. You cannot have a cycle of abuse without actually existing abusers. That sounds simple, which is why so many academics hate it. When scholars defend Avital—or "complicate the narrative," as we like to say—in part this is because we cannot stand believing what most people believe. The need to feel smarter is deep. Intelligence is a hungry god.

Ronell was suspended for an academic year, then reinstated.

One of your last events before you leave your first lectureship is to chair a discussion between two poets whose works held you during lockdown.

Kayo Chingonyi writes in "interior w/ceiling fan,"

> let me be this unguarded always
> speaking without need for words
> because breath is the oldest language
> any of us know

When senior colleagues learn you are leaving, you are sometimes asked why.

Sometimes you say, it's a promotion, my new post, an exciting opportunity for me.

Other times you say, I didn't like the way I was changing.

Mary Jean Chan writes in "A Hurry of English":

> What does it say about me, this obsession written in a lan-
> guage I never chose? My desires dressed themselves in a hurry
> of English to avoid my mother's gaze. How I typed "Shake-
> speare," then "homoeroticism + Shakespeare" into Google,
> over and over. My mother did not understand the difference
> between English words, so she let me be. A public history
> seeps into the body, the way tea leaves soak up the scent of a
> fridge. An odourless room is not necessarily without trauma.
> We must interrogate the walls. My skin is yellow because it
> must. Love is kind because it must. Admit it, aloud.

When Chan reads aloud, you are overwhelmed by how tired you
have been, how tired you are. You long for the clarity with which
Chan speaks.

When you try to articulate that the history of your curiosity is that
of your desire is that of your dream is that of your hope is that of
your thriving is that of your survival, you can't find your footing,
your body feels thin on the ground. You keep squinting at the
screen. You are not seeing well.

In the last two years of your first lectureship, you start to develop what feels like a visual obsession.

You see white.

Such as the time you open a chain of internal emails celebrating the department's inclusivity. The word, made senseless, lodges in your skull, ballooning white and filling your vision.

White sends you into fitful spirals; sometimes with logorrhea, sometimes choking on your own spit. Your anxiety around teaching grows. You thought, for a while, you had adapted to embarrassing yourself on the job, but you start to dread entering the classroom.

You lose a thread of thought, you lose language, and it's just white. White patting itself on the back, white foaming at the mouth about how supportive a white white is—how lucky white we are, but even you, especially you, you who won't attend mandatory Research Day to white celebrate our spectacular white fruits of our white labor, our luminous research, our life's white work that you, you don't really seem to understand, as you won't even join in on our Christmas games of sharing baby photos and guessing who's white.

You have only white to say; you must project through your mask.

The teaching itself almost always goes fine. Your students remain your hope, even when they read about racial violence, and there's always at least one who finds they must say, I just don't believe that would actually happen in real life. I would never do something like that. I don't know anyone who would do something like that. People are good.

The instructor is not a bad person, your senior colleague counters. You are reporting on a student's account of a postgraduate seminar on Baldwin, the discussion consumed by two white women expressing how guilty Baldwin made them feel as figurative daughters of slaveholders.

No one is saying anyone is a bad person, you say, I don't think that's what the student is suggesting.

You ask your student what the moderation was like.

Your student says, The instructor just let them go on, if that's what you mean. She told the white women they were brave.

The instructor is not a bad person, your senior colleague counters. You are reporting on a student's account of a postgraduate seminar on ZZ Packer, the discussion consumed by the white instructor inviting her almost entirely white students'—all save one—liberal use of the *N*-word.

No one is saying, you say—and you are lost to the blank page. You open and close your mouth. You emit white noise.

You apologize to your student. Sometimes they have been in your class; sometimes they have found you through word of mouth. None of these meetings are documentable hours for your workload.

Your student says, I don't think this is the right place for me.

Your fear bleaches; your fear deepens white.

You don't dwell on each shooting anymore. Not the way you feel Mother Emanuel. Not the way you can't read too much about Atlanta.

Lately, the books people are recommending to you are often by contemporary authors who died young. You don't know what to make of this phenomenon and you don't want to think of the authors and the books in this way, but you keep a separate stack, reading cautiously, and so somewhat distractedly, skipping between books, always with something on in the background.

Your show of choice is old episodes of <심야괴담회>, seasons you binged with your parents during trips home, your mother getting up every five minutes, your dad falling asleep, both natural responses to ghost stories for people who don't particularly enjoy ghost stories. You've seen the title translated in two ways, *Midnight Horror Story* or *Late Night Ghost Talk*. You prefer the slight stiltedness of the latter.

One episode tells the story of a father and son driving home from a distant relative's funeral. It was a quiet evening on the road, just their car and another behind them for miles. Together, the two cars entered a long tunnel cutting through a mountain.

They drove for some time, their headlights cutting white through the strangely tinctured dimness of the tunnel. Suddenly the car behind began flashing their lights. Then they began to honk wildly. The father tried slowing down, speeding up, but the car behind kept pace, blaring their horn and driving erratically, too fast, too close, swerving into the other lane as if they might try to overtake them but never actually doing so. The tunnel went on and on, the noise of the horn resounding, father and son trapped in time expanded.

But the tunnel did end with the promise of stars above. As both cars shot out into the open air, the horn ceased. For the father, the space carved into him by relief filled instantly with fury. He hit the brakes hard, forcing the car behind him to stop, too. He ordered his son to stay in the car, slamming the door as he got out.

The father squared his shoulders and approached the other car, his throat loaded with so many words—only to find them disperse at the sight of a lone young woman crying at the wheel.

She was shaking so badly that at first the father could barely make out that the woman was apologizing. So much so that the father told her to stop, shush, just tell him what happened.

"There was something on your car," she said. "Up on the roof. At first I thought it was an animal, but it just didn't look right. It didn't feel right. It didn't feel right, the thing on your car. When I turned on my high beams, I saw it was a woman with long dark hair, crouching there. She was clawing at the roof, like she was trying to get in."

Your recollection of the story grows hazier from here. Once the father and son got home, there may have been a mother with a mixture of salt and red mung beans. Maybe not a mother, maybe a shaman. There was definitely salt and red mung beans involved. There almost always is. It's possible father and son drove around for a little while, stopping by a public place before going home. Your own mother taught you that this is another way to shake off spirits.

What you do remember is that initially the father didn't tell his young son anything. He just got back in their car and kept driving for a while. It was years later, when the son was more grown, that his father revealed what had happened, what the other driver had said that night at the end of the tunnel and, too, that the father had found long claw marks atop his car, cutting through the paintwork, digging up ridges in the metal beneath.

What stays with you is that the end of the story had no further mention of the other driver, the woman who had tried her best to scare off some terrible spirit. You fear most what became of her, left shaking and crying, stopped at the wide mouth of the tunnel, alone.

You were about half your age when you had to take a class called Theory of Knowledge. It was taught by a man who looked ancient to you then, whose lessons almost always derailed into a diatribe against the innate goodness of human beings.

He once posed what he called a thought experiment: Imagine the last glass of water on earth, he said, set between you and another person. It can be the person you think you love most in the world. It can be the person who you think loves you most in the world. That other person is guaranteed to fight you to the death for that last glass of water. They would rather you die than give up that last glass of water for you. That other person will kill you for it. No matter who it is sitting across from you, they would rather murder you.

It was the first time you spoke up to him. The sacrifice of parents. Mothers saving their babies. The victims of Columbine. 9/11. These were your touchstones, then. You weren't just trying to point out that in nature and nurture, at every terrible turn of history, kindness endures; you didn't have the language yet, but you were also trying to articulate how violent it felt for him to try to teach you not to trust in other people, to stop believing in your capacity to love and be loved.

He cut you off. He scoffed. He rolled his eyes. He waved you off with his hands. He moved on to what was ostensibly another subject.

He gave you a B-minus on a major presentation after that. When you asked him to explain your grade, he said, "You just didn't sparkle." He died the year after you took his class, and it was only then that you learned how sick he was while he was teaching.

And what of the woman atop the car? Who will braid her long dark hair? Who will file down her deathly nails and coo as she grits her teeth against the scraping of metal?

You concede you can't change the system from within, but you propose you can change relative positions. You propose you can make the important parts of yourself indelible.

What if you keep inching forward from the belly?

What if you can look out from the open mouth?

Comforting a girl half your age, you find yourself repeating words you have heard from the women who held you.

MOTHER slowly unhinges her jaw. She speaks but the sound comes from deep inside her.

But what if you are out of thick salt? What if you have no dried red mung beans in storage, no peach or cinnamon branches nearby? What if you forget sacred words, or the prayers do not come from you, exact?

Tree, ah, me, get on fire, coffin, count sound, violet flesh.

Do not give in entirely to fear. The memory of what is sacred is sacred, too. Inside you more blessed by the collapsing of unspeakable things and time.

DAUGHTER, you are protected.

DAUGHTER, you are safe.

You wish her home. You wish her mother waiting. Home, where she will tell her mother what happened.

We Are Moving to America

1. HOT CAR

This is a recurring nightmare: You are a baby when daddy leaves you in a hot car. What you remember is green and gold light beyond the window and the slap of our mother's cold, hard hand. In the kitchen, she throws a glass at daddy and misses. Just a baby, our mother says. Take the baby to the shaman, daddy says. Our mother turns to you and her face is like glass. She leaves the room, but you can hear her weeping.

Daddy draws near. He hesitates before splaying his hand atop your head. You lean into his touch and close your eyes. You don't see his face as he leans down to whisper,

> you are not my child
>
> you are a snake

2. PIG BIG

You steal a dream. You eavesdrop on the prettiest girl in class telling her best friend about a dream she had about a giant pig, a pig big enough to span the city. As she shouted in terror at the city-big pig, the pig snorted deeply, and she was swept up like a dust particle into the pig's nostril. On your way to the airport, you relay this dream to our mother, but you say you dreamt it, you say the dream is yours. Our mother is so happy. You feel you've done the right thing because our mother is so happy and she tells you to tell her the dream again and again. You tell our mother your dream three times. You are naming a beast you will never understand. You say, I'm going to miss my best friend the most, naming the prettiest girl in your class. Everything's going to be better in America, our mother says. In America, you grow fat. You have one friend. Her name is Jessica. She is fatter than you. You are her only friend, too. You are sitting on the floor of your school gymnasium, home of the Longstreet Road Indians. All the pretty girls are on the bleachers with the pretty boys. You are supposed to be jumping rope, but the gym teacher is busy with the boom box. I have a secret, you whisper to Jessica. On the radio, Larry Sprinkle says Floyd replaced his eye wall this morning. This can occur multiple times in intense hurricanes. During this period, the hurricane may level off or weaken, but then gain strength as the outer eye wall contracts inward, replacing the old inner eye wall, leaving a larger core with a larger wind field. Jessica breathes into your ear. Do you eat dogs? You breathe into her ear.   You write a novel.

3. DREAM BABY

She says that you were born without a dream, but the baby lost to her before you was foretold by a ginseng flower. When you spot a ginseng, you have to claim it out loud for it to be yours. It's not enough to see it first. You have to shout about it. You have to call down from the mountains that you have seen the spirit. I HAVE SEEN THE SPIRIT. These are the words. No, that's not right. 심봤다. These are the words. And they mean something else. For months, she didn't even realize she was pregnant with you. By the time she found out, she couldn't remember a single dream she'd had to foretell your coming. It was only after so much worrying she decided you had been there, too, in that first dream, because even though she didn't get to unearth the precious root, she saw the flower. My first baby was the root, our mother says, but you are the flower.

4. THE BODY (WE ARE MOVING TO AMERICA)

They say, Have you no allegiance to the Viking King who stained his teeth with blueberries to bring himself a little closer to Mary, Mother of God? He said, "A snake is only ever a snake. As a kid, I had a deathly, phobic fear of snakes. I can tell you when it stopped. I was nine and my old man decided to take me to a pet store to get one. Told me to stick my hand in a tank of babies and grab mine, so I did." We tie him down with ropes spun from our hair. We are not careful with our incisions, but we speak the incantation tenderly:

> eyes leave you
>
> eyes leave you
>
> eyes leave you

There is more blood than we can cup in our hands. The Viking King is as wide as the double doors of his church. Our temple has no doors, only rock formations and earthen tunnels that lead to burrows beneath tall trees, deep where we make our beds shared with the bones of animal things: our sisters before us, and red foxes, and white rabbits, and a black bear who lost her cubs and so never woke up for spring. We have seen it up there, the domain of the Viking King. It is loud and it has the sun. We came to understand we are moving to America only when we are hurt enough for them to taste our tears are salted, too, our blood just as tinctured with minerals. There is little light, but down here we can crystallize, and in the damp dark of his head where his eyes used to be we plant mushrooms that look like the heads of snakes and know we will not   be   turned   to   gold.

정 [Mother's Tongue]

Before my still-new job, my first lectureship, I used to go home for the summer to help my parents at their ice-cream store. My dad has a bad knee and rough, clumsy hands. For nearly twenty years now, he has churned butterfat of the highest order and has moved stacks of three-gallon buckets of ice cream in a way that makes me think of other fathers I have seen lift toddlers into the air like their children weigh nothing to them.[1] Lately, I find myself worrying that my dad might die with his hands clenched in fear, in that place we call home with so much to fear, taking fistfuls of things he can't speak of with him. Lately, I find myself mouthing something like prayer to no god in particular, awake in the dark: When his time comes, please let my father go with his hands resting open.

I ask and I ask no god in particular: Has my father not made enough ice cream?[2]

---

1 If I were writing a novel, I would write about the glug of the ice-cream machine, the sigh of the dark and boxy walk-in freezer, lingering on the way my father slams the heavy buckets down onto the metal counter, not from anger but exhaustion, his handling of these frozen, child-sized masses so unlike that of a father standing in green and gold light in some wide-open space, holding his child up to the blue on high.

2 Back home, it's not rare to encounter those who see my face and want to convert me. One such white man, flanked by two white women who would not meet my eyes, interrupted me eating with two Black friends at some outdoor food court and spoke only to me. He told me that Buddha himself said that he is not the way. I had made no mention of my mother's mother, the only devout Buddhist I knew. My father's parents were Catholic. What I remember of them is their disinterest in me and deep hatred of my mother. To this day, when she rarely speaks of them, my mother can't help but grit her teeth, then cry anyway.

People who don't know often assume that ice cream is easy work, smooth and sweet. But it is unrelenting.[3] Ice cream means hard labor. Ice cream means proud Americans who can be cruel when hungry, crueler still when bloated full.[4] My dad works the store alone most days because my mom has developed a hand tremor. It embarrasses her as much as it impedes her scooping or waffle-cone-baking, making each interaction with customers that much more challenging, from fear that she will drop someone's order, their change, or that the sight of her tremors alone will upset or offend, all alongside the living anxiety of handling English.[5] And there is,

---

3   I grit my teeth thinking of the customer who lectured my father about service with a smile, wagging his finger in my father's face, working himself up to spitting mad about how it was my father's job to serve with a smile, especially at an ice-cream store, which is supposed to be a happy place. I asked my father why he didn't say anything, why he didn't fight back, but I also wondered, What if the white man had a gun? What if he comes back with one?

4   I feel some tinge of irritation thinking of the customer who comes in reeking of fish and garlic from a neighboring restaurant but sniffs the air at our store's threshold, cringes, then says, Y'all been eating Chinese food? As she is paying, she lectures my mother about MSG. She is a regular. In the months-turned-years to come, the white woman will never, not once, wear a mask. But what makes me actually grit my teeth as I write is not the thought of her maskless, but of those who would see her as decidedly beneath them, all the while asking me in the most simpering tone, And how are your parents doing?—every time like my parents are dying all the time, just perpetually dying, not because of an unprecedented global pandemic but because my parents work in food service. People who have never had to work for money or have not had to work for money for a long, long time, I hope someone draws deep from the well to spit in everything they ever eat.

5   My mother often says that the way English makes her feel stupid makes her want to crawl into a hole and die. I think about how this expression exists in both English and Korean. I wonder in what language people aim to climb high and die. For example, the inability to express what I feel and mean makes me want to climb a mountain and die.

too, the fact that my mother is shrinking.[6] Not in some fairy-tale way.[7] Something to do with old age and bone density, something to do with how, when and where she was growing up, red meat was as precious as gold.[8] I should have become a doctor, the life-saving and good-money-making kind.

I am an immigrant twice over. 정 is a self-diagnosis of a need to interrogate my first-generation Korean American identity as a means to survive British academia. I don't understand why, a senior colleague says, you are struggling so much to do what is an essential part of the job. In light of a global pandemic, two senior colleagues and I are holding a meeting about my research productivity on Skype. These heavenly line boats are representing the department's growing concern that I will not produce a suitable piece of research for institutional approval.

In Korean, there is a word for those who hold a position senior to yours, formally in title and/or informally through experience, the latter holding more weight in many ways. It is a word for those who have supposedly been where you are, have supposedly done what you are doing, and therefore know better—perhaps even are better, ascended beings. It is a word I came to understand more fully through Korean dramas, through plot points involving a junior colleague who, unfailingly, even in the face of what appears to be unbearable injustice and harm to themselves, must somehow meet

---

6   And of my mother's many dreams, one was that I would grow to be my father's height, approximately five-foot-seven, but I am approximately five inches short and I didn't get into Harvard.

7   If I were writing a fairy tale, I would write about how my mother can touch fire, hold it to her fingers. I would title it "독한년."

8   정 is a fairy tale.

the demands of a senior colleague, ultimately for the greater good of their shared profession and/or workplace and/or existence in general. This Korean word can be phonetically translated as "line boat." There is a Korean saying about how one must revere and serve line boats as one would the heavens.

I need to produce a six-thousand-word essay based on my doctoral research. I am not doing a good job of staying on topic. I am not doing a good job of holding my space. I am crying. I'm sorry, I say, I'm just so tired. 정 has many symptoms, one such being 몸살. I do not have it in me to try again to fully explain to my heavenly line boats what I mean when I say I am tired. It is March 2020, my second year on the job. I am recovering from what I must assume is just a cold and I am having a difficult time comprehending what is this space I am occupying, precisely, professionally. In this space, we are three heads: two heavenly line boat 대가리들, and mine bobbing in and out as I reach for tissues. I am wondering if the sound of me blowing my nose is made grosser by the faint static and echo, the strange resonance of Wi-Fi, as gross as I feel. Our connections keep acting up and/or cutting out. I am wondering if I heard right, a heavenly line boat 대가리 asking me if the issue is that I don't actually want to do research, that I don't actually want to write. Why else would I not be able to produce a six-thousand-word essay? The heavenly line boat 대가리 says we ask our MA students to write six-thousand-word essays all the time. (I feel we must be speaking in tongues. I have grown so tired of the salted taste of my own snot.) The other heavenly line boat 대가리 is quiet. None of us want to have our heads here, in this space and time, projecting and enunciating for the camera.

I am lucky to have my position on three-year probation: a full-time permanent contract that accounts for research. Theoretically, I am paid, in part, to write. (It shouldn't be so hard, I know. And it feels so shameful to try to explain why it is.) In the UK, the Research Excellence Framework (REF) assesses the quality of research in higher education institutions and determines how public funding for research is allocated. In essence, it tasks academics to produce standardized, institutionally approved research. As an Early-Career Researcher, I am minimally tasked to produce one REF-able output for my institution. (One, just one. What is wrong with me?) The REF-ability of a piece of output is measured by the output's IMPACT. I am told that the short scholarly article I have to my name is nice, but not REF-able because it is too short. The length of one's output is perhaps related to IMPACT. I need a REF-able output that will earn many stars for IMPACT,[9] or I'm not quite sure what would happen to me.

I am threatened by the reality that junior academics like me are often forced onto what is known as teaching-only contracts. When I say I am threatened, I mean expressly so. In other words, I am repeatedly told by another heavenly line boat that this shameful thing of a teaching-only contract will happen to me. It is a festering open secret that a teaching-only contract classes one as a second-rate academic. "Teaching," I'm starting to understand, is something of a dirty word in academia.

"Book," on the other hand, is beloved. A book makes for an excellent REF-able output. A book is double-weighted. A book counts twice.

If 정 is a book, it would be 33,333 words long, divided equally into three sections:[10]

---

9   IMPACT is written in all caps and is measured by stars; our research is measured by stars.

10   정 is a lie. 정 is going to be much longer than that. And real messy. You'll see.

I. 정 들어진다, 정 떨어진다: 2018–2019
    i. Autumn
    ii. Spring
    iii. Summer
II. 미운정: 2019–2020
    i. Autumn
    ii. Spring
    iii. Summer
III. 고은정
    i. Going forward, I
    ii. would (strongly; use this word as necessary) encourage
    iii. you to

I am not sure if this outline means anything and/or if it is an outright lie. I wrote it for a proposal I put together too carelessly for a contest promising the prize of a book publication.[11] I was desperate. I am desperate.

The untranslatability of 정 is often mentioned as an integral part of Korean culture.

정 asserts that English is multiplicitous and at its best in symbiosis with another language.

정 approaches fragmentation as a means of mending my broken Korean through my practice of English.

I was born in Seoul and immigrated to rural North Carolina at the age of seven. I was meant to learn English from my second-generation

---

11   I did not make it past the first round, but one of my former students was a finalist and she wrote to say she thought of me and to thank me for my support.

cousins who told me I used bad words because I went to public school with Black kids. My cousins said, Black kids say words like "shut up" and "H-E-DOUBLE-HOCKEY-STICKS." My cousins said, Black kids are going to hell. This is what they learned at their private Catholic school. (It's OK to say hell when you need to state that Black kids are going to hell; this part is silent.) My youngest aunt liked to beat me whenever she felt my parents were ripping her off for looking after me. She liked to say I was like a snake. 독한년. 뱀같은년. Poisonous and/or venomous, it was not so much about specificity. My uncle liked to watch. When my parents were working too late to come pick me up, he was the one to drive me home. Sometimes, at the end of our silent ride, he would tell me without looking at me, You need to learn when to shut your mouth, you need to learn to be less selfish. I often begged my mom to stop leaving me with them, but she wanted to impress upon me the importance of family.

I hold a Ph.D. in the New Southern Gothic from the University of Manchester, where I studied under white men who praised my ability to write a Black voice.[12] But is it really salable to write about the Civil War, the KKK? they posed. Why is there an ice-cream store in the swamp? Life in the New South wasn't all that bad. Have you watched *Gone With the Wind*? Have you read Faulkner? Have you tried writing Korean stories?

The New Southern Gothic is a flimsy phrase. What I mean is that I read Yusef Komunyakaa's *Neon Vernacular* (1993) as a study of the Southern Gothic in solidarity with the Black Lives Matter movement. What I mean is that I did try reading Faulkner and O'Connor and all those good country people and sure as heck they

---

12 I wish I had asked what this meant, exactly. I wish I had asked more questions myself, but I was trying too hard to offer answers.

sure are great, but I just didn't want to lie for tens of thousands of words about such writers speaking profoundly to what home means to me. What I mean is that sometime in the late 1990s or possibly early 2000s, when I was much too young for Komunyakaa's words, if I hadn't by pure chance asked my mother if I could buy this book of poetry (1) because the cover had a quiet buzzing silver & gold & bronze muted by a wash of sickly green, a somehow loving and somehow angry collage of city life between the gold & bronze full of more jagged cars than good city people, a half-blind eye at the center of it all, with the hands of time protruding from the pupil, and (2) because the author's name seemed just as strange if not stranger than mine in these united states,[13] I may never have started writing my first novel about an ice-cream store built shortly after the American Civil War because I needed to better understand how home feels to me. 정 is home.

I have yet to finish the novel I submitted as a part of my doctoral thesis.

I have been unworking my first novel for five years.

My novel will not be published in time for this REF cycle.

In "Work," Yusef Komunyakaa writes:

I won't look. The engine

---

13   I have learned to hold my Korean name close in fear of old hurts from when I was young. When I could better read Komunyakaa's words, I was entering my twenties. It was the summer I fell in love with a grown woman from New York. Beneath the frenetic markings for my doctoral thesis, I can still make out the sections I marked to share with her from "Songs for My Father" and "Faith Healer."

Pulls me like a dare.
Scent of honeysuckle
Sings black sap through mystery,
Taboo, law, creed, what kills
A fire that is its own heart
Burning open the mouth.[14]

In "The Most Delicious You in the Whole World," Kim Hyesoon writes:

Pig9 Please raise and eat me
Pig9 Please cry after eating me
Pig9 I'll give birth to piglets
Pig9 Please say for once that you had a sad life
Pig9 Please wrap me up well and prepare me for a meal
Pig9 Please hang my intestines on a string
Pig9 Please don't throw away any part of me
Pig9 Please don't burp so loudly

May I call this delicious thing You?
May I gently-gently lovingly gnaw on you?[15]

Yusef Komunyakaa's is the poetry I raised myself with; Kim Hyesoon's is the poetry I should have been raised with. 정 is an allegiance to both, at once.

What I remember of finding Kim Hyesoon's works is that it was a year or two before I got my job and I felt the title, *I'm OK, I'm PIG!*, like someone punching me in the stomach. I remember it had to be

14   Yusef Komunyakaa, *Neon Vernacular* (Wesleyan University Press, 1993), pp. 11–12.

15   Kim Hyesoon, *I'm OK, I'm PIG!*, trans. by Don Mee Choi (Bloodaxe Books, 2014), pp. 101–102.

2016 or 2017, because I was trying to explain to my husband why I was so struck by the title and I started crying and my husband assumed I was just stressed from the job hunt. (He was always reassuring me that I would finish my book and find a job soon.) I wrote a lecture for my MA students trying to speak to this feeling and 정 is the joy of teaching because it was one of my students who thought to invite me when Kim Hyesoon and Don Mee Choi came to do a reading in London in May 2019 and I got to hold Kim Hyesoon's hand and blubber mostly nonsense at her in a mix of Korean and English.[16] All the white and gray and glass of the Southbank venue was too much for me. I also used Don Mee Choi's name incorrectly when trying to speak to her in Korean and she said, It's OK, it's OK, just speak English.[17] At some point, I must have conveyed in some form my intense desire to work with her. She said, Just email me, email me, but I haven't.

When I shared an abstract of my lecture on feeling OK and feeling PIG! with a heavenly line boat, they kept referring to Kim Hyesoon as "your poet," using phrases such as, "I know you're excited about your poet, but," growing more and more agitated by my phrase "whitewashing of witchcraft." I love *The Craft*, my heavenly line boat says, then quotes Audre Lorde, telling me to put down the master's tools. I smile and I hold it. 정 is that encounters like this take me right back to that moment when my cousins and I gathered before my uncle as he bit into some American fruit or vegetable

---

16　교수님, 죄송합니다. 하지만, when your bright and shining daughter spoke so casually of handling toxic materials known to cause serious illness or death for her art, I would just like you to know that I felt very—I felt, very, as the daughter of a mother who instilled in me deep, had to, an animal fear of unjust sickness, unjust death. I felt, very. I hope you'll understand.

17　또 한번 죄송합니다.

I hadn't seen before. How is it? I asked. What does it taste like? What's the word? my uncle said, looking past us to try to find it. It's very, he said, then looked right at me. 시다, 셔. Did he mean sour? Did he mean tart? I say both. I say, Sour? Tart? No, my uncle says, no. He studied the victual and took another bite, chewed slowly, then swallowed. 써, he said, looking at me again. Bitter, I said. You mean bitter. No, he said, looking away from me and grimacing. My cousins snickered, the younger one saying, You don't even know Korean.

Sometimes I fear I was cruel to my cousins in kind. I remember my fury that they hadn't learned about the 6.25 전쟁, not even as the 한국 전쟁, knowing then the significance of these words by heart and feeling the gravity all through me and beyond me in a way I thought then would surely be unending. I remember lecturing my cousins about the line that cuts through our country on every map, not just the Korean ones, but the American ones, too. Did you never notice? Did you never ask why? Don't you care where we come from, where I just came from and wish, so badly, I could go back to? Don't you care what was done to us? I remember I wanted to go back, then, in those days, more than anything, I wanted to go home, and at some point, even a feeling like wanting to go home can stop, at least for a while.[18] I remember replicating the punishments of my teachers in Korea, making my American cousins sit on their knees, arms raised, or wrapping their knuckles with my ruler, my Korean ruler, the one I brought from Korea. I was desperate to be proud of my Korean kind of power as the oldest. I was desperate to feel proud before them.[19]

---

18 And you may not let it come back for a long, long time. There will be many reasons, all difficult to explain, especially cumulatively.

19 Once, just as my aunt had us sit down for a meal, I noticed a hair in my soup. It was a clear soup and the hair was long and black, undulating and floating in the cen-

정 is that I remember things like this and I carry them with me and I feel further sour, tart, and bitter but can't and/or don't really want to put into words what I think about it and how it makes me feel. I am conscious that maybe I'm doing that here. 정 is maybe doing.

정 is also good intention and bad language.

정 is also bad intention and good language.

정 is rarely bad intention and bad language.

정 is often good intention and good language.

I try to teach my students the importance of unlearning, and that is 정, too. Alexander Chee writes in "How to Unlearn Everything," "If I'm helping students cross boundaries, I urge them to look at the ones they find within. I also urge them to set them for themselves."[20]

---

ter of the white bowl. I plucked it out quickly and shook my hand free of it. I knew I wasn't supposed to say anything. I didn't say anything. But they were watching me. And it was my uncle who shouted at me first. Who do you think is going to clean that up? You thoughtless, ungrateful child. Find it and pick it up, he said. He watched me crouch, watched me shift around slowly, patting the floor as I moved, in case I could feel for the strand of hair that could be missed by sight alone. You won't find it like that, he said. Stop being lazy. Get down on your hands and knees and look properly. Don't you dare get up until you clean up your mess. I crawled, looking for the hair. I crawled until I found it, long and dark, wet and slightly coiled. My uncle continued to shout orders until I disposed of the hair. I watched it flutter briefly in the air as I dropped it into the trash. I stood there, head bowed and hands clasped, until I was told to rejoin the table. As I sat down, the older of my cousins bent from his seat, his hand pinching at something on the floor. His sister giggled. My aunt clicked her tongue. The older of my cousins held up a long black hair. Dad, dad, look, he said, She only pretended to find one. She's a liar.

20   Alexander Chee, "How to Unlearn Everything: When It Comes to Writing the

My official job title is Lecturer in Creative and Critical Writing. I was hired in September 2018. In my interview, a panelist stated that the college was trying to make the staff body look more like the student body. My first day on the job, another panelist informed me that I was the second-choice candidate, that the award-winning novelist the rest of the hiring committee had been desperate to obtain couldn't be bothered to do the amount of teaching required of a junior academic.

정 is my want to hold the hands of the award-winning novelist and thank them for saving my life.

But I was the only one who fought for you, the panelist, now a heavenly line boat, said. I was the one who convinced the others that we could put you to work.

정 is my capacity to smile and tell all the heavenly line boats, This is my dream job, and mean it.

This is my dream job. I enter with two years remaining in the current four-year REF cycle.

In my very first research productivity meeting, three weeks or so into the job, I find myself puzzled by needing to explain to my heavenly line boats that I cannot ask my agent to publish my novel faster. I stumble over the politest, most deferential way to say that's not how it works. Over my first year, I come to understand that it is a great disappointment to my department, to my institution, perhaps even a failing (of the innate kind; this part is silent) on my part, that my novel will not be published in time as a REF-able output. I am told to publish an eight-thousand-word novel extract somewhere like *The New Yorker* (but obviously not *The New Yorker*; this part is silent). I am told if all else fails, a personal website or maybe a blog would need to be built upon which to throw up my novel. I publish an eight-thousand-word novel extract with a long-standing independent literary journal in America. For months, even after publication, I reread the kind acceptance note from the editor when I need to remember I am not my dream job.

It is not easy to remember.

Time shifts and I am told my extract is not REF-able. I am (gently-gently) told my writing is atmospheric. I am (gently-gently) told I write like Toni Morrison. I am told that my three-hundred-word REF narrative to accompany my piece reads like something written by a student; endearing, but not REF-able.[21] My uterus bleeds for eight weeks. I call my GP. The next available appointment through the National Health Service that fits with my work schedule is three months away. I was told (by my white, blond, and blue-eyed British American husband; this part is silent but I desperately wish we, he and I, were having this conversation with you in person at the surgery[22]) that you have morning appointments for urgent cases

---

21 The REF narrative aims to explain how and why a practice-based, creative work constitutes formal, academic research.

22 And I have learned these conversations are often best served when I stand a half step behind my husband and let him do all the talking for me and do not, under any circumstances, interject unless my husband speaks directly to me first, leaving room for the possibility that my English is perhaps not good enough to participate fully in these conversations. It's November, nearly two months into my still-new job, and it's Thanksgiving in a white British American household. I am seated in what I

(such as that time my husband found a small bump on his hand; such as the time my husband had a lingering cough). Please, I say, I am feeling very tired and hardly have the energy to do anything. I have been bleeding for eight weeks, I reiterate, and add (please, I'm so scared; this part is silent and instead find myself articulating, calmly, reservedly, that), I suspect this issue is exacerbated by the birth control implant in my arm. The receptionist says that birth control issues do not qualify for an emergency appointment. My heavenly line boats tell me I need to produce a REF-able academic essay based on my Ph.D. work over Christmas break.

I never had a strong sense of time, but I fear I am losing it completely. When I am no longer sure that I can write not like a student but

---

come to realize is the Asian corner, but to the other, largely British guests must be the Chinese corner. There is me, another Korean woman, and a Vietnamese woman. We are the extent of the color here, three whole of us at least, at least for those who see color. Actually, seated between me and the Vietnamese woman is her partner, a white American man. What is most certain is that we are all pond jumpers here. I don't know who exactly decided to seat me between the coupling "just like" mine, but I want to pluck three hairs from my head to stir into their soup: obviously one for me, one for the Vietnamese woman, and one for the other Korean woman. I know what they will say: Oh, but you all have and/or are doing Ph.D.s! I am not contributing enough to the general conversation and, furthermore, I am certainly failing in my intended purpose to rally my corner to join in on the general conversation. At one point, the Vietnamese woman's partner kindly asks me about my new job, but I think I say "Cassandra" instead of "Vanessa" when talking about the dumbwaiter, the dumbwaiter, the only thing I can recall and speak to about my job in this moment and I'm just so fucking tired so I keep stuffing my face and I hardly feel bad at all when the Vietnamese woman is doing most of the talking from our corner. "My parents are refugees," I can hear her saying in just the right way. I hardly feel bad at all because, honestly, I'm just really grateful it's not me this time. Occasionally I glance across no-man's-land to my white, blond, and blue-eyed British American husband, who smiles to reassure himself I am coping OK, and I wonder if he ever thinks: I have grown tired of the black fibrous tendrils in her soups. 정 is Thanksgiving.

like a real academic, a most rare heavenly line boat who becomes a friend (placing me on equal footing and helping me even when it is at risk to herself) drafts and edits an email with me to send to other heavenly line boats:

January 24, 2020

Dear Heavenly Line Boats,

I appreciate the time you have both taken helping me think through my REF submission and I am sorry to report that I won't be able to submit an essay to you, as suggested, by the end of this month. On reflection, I don't feel that it was ever realistic to think that I would come up with an essay in a matter of a few weeks, during a period that included teaching and a busy Christmas break, and only a week or so free of those commitments. In addition, I am now contending with a considerable marking burden alongside a full teaching load.

If I had completed research for an essay, this may have been more realistic, though still pretty ambitious, but as you know I have been working on my novel, and building on my Ph.D. material would need careful and thorough consideration of new contributions to my subject. Given that scholarly work typically takes months if not years to germinate, it seems unlikely that any piece completed in this short timescale would reach the standard required by the REF committee.

I feel I am operating from a place of anxiety and fear, and that this has been detrimental to my productivity. I will certainly continue trying to publish a REF output in time for this cycle, but I need to be able to research and write on my own terms and cannot commit to the form this will take or meet a deadline.

Thank you again for your support.

Best wishes,
Jodie

I want to be clear that I am grateful. I want to be clear that I admire all my heavenly line boats and the hard work they do and I want to be clear that I understand they themselves are being charged with tasks they may not necessarily believe in. I want to be clear that all my heavenly line boats have been excellent, double-weighted mentors for me. I want to be clear that I can attest to the IMPACT they have had on my still-new dream job. I would count every single one of them twice, each, easily. They are as good as books to me.[23] I want to be clear that I couldn't have endured my dream job even for this long without mentors, mentors who got me here and keep me here (even if and/or especially when I am unwell), mentors who rampage on Twitter when I forget my own anger and/or when I am too scared to resist:

1. The REF is gross! It's moronic and it's bad for everyone. That's my thought for the day.
2. I mean, it's harmful, corrosive, & divisive. But it's also embarrassing; it makes me cringe, this denigration of the humanities & critique, this capitulation of the language that *we* have to describe the world, to the inappropriate metrics of science & social science
3. the language of "methodology" and "findings" is not appropriate to a literary essay; why are we having to pretend it is, even while knowing and acknowledging that it is not?

---

23 If I could, I would get them the good stars, four?, five?, I don't know what the maximum number of stars REF gives is, but I would get all the stars, I would get all the stars I could for them.

4. it matters, this resigned application of the wrong language to literary writing; it makes writers seem like slightly dappy researchers; and even if we all profess to "know" the REF is bullshit, the consistent application of wrong metrics to art is profoundly damaging

5. & the fact is that, regardless of how well given departments and individuals handle the universally hated REF process, it inevitably reproduces inequalities & thrives on preexisting power structures

6. not least because, in order to do the REF, one has to fall in line with the assumption that different kinds of work have to defer to a single (& highly positivist) measure of success

7. & one has to go along with the fiction that using language instrumentally is OK as long as we all know it's instrumental

8. but that is not true; large swathes of critical inquiry are *about* language, about refusing certain kinds of language, & about refusing a purely instrumental & technocratic use of language

9. & many creative endeavours are likewise about refusing certain language games, & creating others

10. & so the grimness of the REF process is exacerbated for creative writers, who find themselves not only having to go along with the moronic & troubling use of language the REF imposes, but also having to explain themselves to the "discipline" of their academic colleagues

11. anyway, I like my job, and I hover between creative and critical and can be an academic with one hat on and a writer with another, but the REF fucks us all up, vote Labour, let's halt the marketisation of universities!

My uterus bleeds for twelve weeks straight. Boris Johnson is PM[24] and every woman I love and admire seems to be intimate with debilitating periods. I think about calling my mom, but she would spend money she can't afford to overnight unidentifiable Korean herbal medicine and a Costco-size bottle of Tylenol to me. The herbal medicine will cost her about the same as the last prescription for her hand tremor, which cost $368 and something cents? (That can't be right.) Why did you send me Tylenol? I will ask her, more annoyed than I have any right to be. She will say Tylenol is cheaper in America and she wouldn't be wrong. Tylenol isn't available in the UK, at least I haven't seen it, but maybe that's because it's just a brand name? I don't know. I'm not the right kind of doctor. If I endure academia, one day I may be able to pay for my parents' health care. I'm so homesick (or, in other words, I have such a profound desire to prolong my parents' lives so that we may have more time together to try to undo some of the harm that has been done unto us by America). I don't call my mother.

March 16, 2020

Dear Heavenly Line Boats,

Thank you for taking the extra time to speak with me today. I really appreciate your ongoing support.

This has been a difficult first REF process for me, but I feel I have made every effort to meet the tasks set for me. Though it is

---

24   I am trying to write what is missing from the ending when my husband calls out from the other room, "Boris has the virus." I'm scared that if he dies, he would become a martyr. It's October 30, 2020, when I am editing this piece with another kind editor. The editor notes here, "He doesn't die."

disappointing that the submission resulted in further edits, I did send my novel to my agent as we discussed. I then placed an 8,000-word extract in a reputable publication, and it is unfortunate that the panel found this to be unsuitable for REF.

I would like to reiterate that I care deeply about my job, including the integrity of my research practice. I do understand that we all have to meet institutional demands, but my aim is to maintain researching and creating on my own terms.

I need to take more assertive measures to make and protect research time. We are pressing forward for a 6,000-word essay publication by September. On reflection, I believe I can share an early draft with you by the end of April. I will be in touch with you.

Thank you again and please stay safe.

All best,
Jodie

I reach out to the only female lecturer of color I have been able to identify and work with in person thus far. She is an external examiner from another institution. She is an award-winning novelist. She has spent over a decade at her institution teaching Creative Writing. The year before we met, she was forced onto a teaching-only contract that explicitly prevents her from applying for any funding opportunities to write.[25] I struggle not to say bad words that make me seem less academic. Over a long lunch we are not meant to have time for, we are both careful with our words. She apologizes for not being the mentor I may have been hoping

---

25   By the time I finish the first published draft of this essay, she's left academia.

for and I can't apologize, in turn, fast enough. Time stirs and I compose emails to her in my head.

In another department, a student writes an open letter to her lecturers in the face of an instructor doubling down when asked by another student to please stop using the *N*-word in the classroom. The writer, Aman Ahluwalia, digs in and goes on to publish an article questioning why our institution enables a highly influential department to be led by a man who openly endorses racism through social media.[26]

In my department, students reach out to me to share similar experiences of racial violence in the classroom. I know what happens if you file a complaint. I know what happens if you don't.

In "Fever," Yusef Komunyakaa writes, "Some nights I lie / Awake, staring into a promised land."[27]

In "Father Is Heavy, What Do I Do?" Kim Hyesoon writes, "엘리엘리" and Don Mee Choi writes, "Eloi, Eloi!" and I read and I hear a fantasy father who says, "일로와, 일로와!"[28] Though I cannot see him clearly, this other father calls to me as my father may have done in another time, in another land altogether, and I feel as if this

---

26   Aman Ahluwalia, "Why Won't Birkbeck Deal With Its Problem of Racist Academic Staff?" *gal-dem*, November 13, 2019. <https://gal-dem.com/why-wont-birkbeck-deal-with-its-problem-of-racist-academic-staff/> [accessed March 27, 2020].

27   Komunyakaa, pp. 24–26.

28   Mary Jean Chan is here, too, who wrote "Conversation with Fantasy Mother" first. Thank our fantasy gods for them, for I, too, have seen that impossibly white cake. But mine was made of ice cream, vanilla through and through. Mary Jean Chan, *Flèche* (Faber, 2019), p. 19.

is what is given to me, the language that is felt, by the women who wrote the words before me.[29]

Out of the blue, my dad sends me a letter, and it really is as if a fairy-tale gift has emerged from the water or fallen from the sky. He began the letter over my last Christmas visit, the night we watched <기생충> together.[30]

정 is a wriggling white many-legged thing that slaps cold and sleek-bellied to your face and squeezes around your eyeball into that soft dark cavity of your skull, eating its way up and up into gray matter until you shout, "Amazing!" and/or muse quietly, "Everyone is a parasite."

정 is the first letter my father has ever written to me. The letter is eleven lines long in Korean. The salutation itself counts as a full line, addressed to his daughter who he is proud of for working so hard for others. I cry with every reading because I can feel the hurt my father lives with and the weight of his love and hope for me. My father is a gifted writer.[31] I wonder if a letter like this could have

---

29 KHS, p. 27.

30 봉준호, <기생충>, CJ 엔터테인먼트, 2019. A Korean reviewer in Korea taught me that Korean titles are not italicized; they, we, use these arrows like open mouths that to me mean less than and equal than. I want to thank them for being the first-ever Korean reader in Korea of my work that I know of. 감사합니다. 걱정해주셔서 감사합니다.

31 He closes the letter by saying he will pray for me to build a happy family with my husband. I wonder if he means happier than ours. I wonder who my father prays to and how. I wonder about the years we spent down the hall from one another, awake in the dark and mouthing at our sadness, sometimes in the same language, sometimes not. We cannot get that time back, and yet, it is ours, is it not? There are things I used to be able to name only in Korean, but I can't name them at all now. For example, the

saved 조승희's life, and so, the lives of his victims. I know this is dangerous thinking but 정 is I think and feel it. Sometimes I can't remember the face of a beloved cousin I grew up with in Korea who, long after I immigrated, came back from mandatory service unable to speak, until he threw himself out his bedroom window and screamed all the way down.

Sometimes I google 조승희 and wonder who else can see the animal fear in his eyes, where kindness must have been, once. And then I can better remember my cousin 정's face. 정 is a Korean death story and so should be set to the ever-present whisper of burning incense, the slow shaking of brass bells and a woman's wailing (mine), both building up in gradual fury and desperation.[32] I remain desperate,

---

little yellow flowers that lined the streets of our apartment in the center of Seoul. Little yellow flowers shaped like stars on the dark wooden branches of tall bushes. I used to stand on my tiptoes to try to reach a topmost star, the petals so bright and yellow in the way we color in the sun as children. Once, my father and I walked along the bushes to catch dragonflies. He'd bought me a bug catcher from the corner store, the plastic handle just long enough for a child to maneuver, the white netting neither too fine nor too durable to pose much risk. The dragonflies looked repulsive up close. The first one I caught on my own struggled so ferociously, tearing enough of the net to tangle its bulbous, iridescent blue and green head in the netting. "Get it out," I demanded to my father. "I'll try," he said. But we both knew what would happen. My dad tried his best with the soft snowy netting, the whirring anger of the dragonfly. The gentlest tug of his broad hand, and I swear there was a snap, maybe a doll-head pop, then the rolling of a jewel to the ground. I was quiet and still as my dad held aloft the ruined body, turning the gone-still wings this way and that against the sun. Death did not dim the prismatic shimmering. It wasn't until my dad rested the ruined body against a branch of yellow flowers that I began to wail with the whole of my body, feeling too many things for any words, no words would do for the way the most minute legs, like scratches of ink on paper, still reached for a little yellow flower, without fully grasping.

32   Here are the base components, you may want these at the end:
ㅇ, ㅇ, ㅇ, ㅇ, ㅇ, ㅇ, ㅇ, ㅇ, ㅇ, ㅇ, ㅏ, ㅑ, ㅓ, ㅕ, ㅗ, ㅛ, ㅜ, ㅠ, ㅡ, ㅣ

endlessly. I write with too many tabs open in the background, one of them still playing a Korean drama I was paying closer attention to until the male protagonist, lover of the female protagonist (who loves the female protagonist very much), reconsiders sending the male antagonist to jail because the male antagonist has a young son. Yes, the male antagonist has tried to outright murder the female protagonist multiple times, but he is actually a very good dad. I have lost the thread of the Korean drama and its many Korean characters, but the stream of language is grounding me to the page and at some point the male protagonist (who loves the female protagonist very much) comforts the male antagonist's son with a sweet and asks the male antagonist's son, "Why aren't you asking me how your dad is doing?" 정 is when the son replies, "Because I miss him."

In "Fever," Yusef Komunyakaa writes,

> I thought I could learn
> To hold these people, love
> Their scary laughter & strength
> With children & animals.
> They accept heartworms
> & infection like God,
> Making me remember
> That if I'd stayed home
> I would've killed
> Someone I love. My father
> Stood apart, wounded
> By what I had seen.
> America, no brass bands,
> No confetti. Please
> Put away your pinwheels
> & tin whistles. What I know

Now can lay open desire
With the right look.

Sometimes I think about the forgiveness that was shown unto 조승희 by the families of his victims and think about the soul of the American South.

정 is an American story, too, so should be set to the crackling drive-through order of a cheeseburger. Unwrap it. Unwrap it some more. Slap the sesame-seeded bun over your genitals. Smoosh the soggy underbun over your asshole. Paste the cheesy patty over your mouth. Lay the warm pickles over your eyes. You are fucking unimpeachable, 지랄새끼야.

In *Hardly War* (2016), Don Mee Choi chants, "I refuse to translate." She declares this over and over and over and over and over, "무궁화꽃이피었습니다."

정 is also a British story, I guess, I propose. I'm part of a union now and we go on strike for fourteen days to disrupt the rotting state of higher education, but we don't protest the REF. In the event of a global pandemic, it is entirely possible that this REF cycle may be canceled. I write this draft. I send it to my mentor friend. She writes back with news that REF is postponed. I feel no relief.

Sara Ahmed writes:

> I think of Lorde: how a poem comes out when she stops what she was doing. I think sometimes you withdraw from a situation— driving a vehicle, being in the driver's seat—to express your commitments. You close the door; stop the car because you need to get something out; you need to get yourself out.

You need to get yourself out; get yourself through.[33]

I compose emails in my head.

Dear Heavenly Line Boats,

Are you both safe and well?

How is your young child? How is your partner?

How are your parents? Are they, like mine, living, but so far away?
Are you close to them in a broken language? Do you ever dog paddle
(for your life) in this language, as I do?

Today, I had a phone tutorial with a student who told me about
speaking to his mother, who is alone in isolation. His mother lived
through the war. His mother said, this is not like the war. When
they dropped the bombs, we could still go dancing.[34]

My student and I kept each other on the line too long, taking our
time trying to comfort one another in our boundaries. He thanked
me for introducing him to books he had never encountered before
in formal education and never would have picked up on his own.
In turn, I encouraged him to consider continuing on with an MA.
I think you'd really enjoy it, I said. He thanked me again and said

---

33   Sara Ahmed, "Complaint and Survival", *feministkilljoys*, March 23, 2020. <https://
feministkilljoys.com/2020/03/23/complaint-and-survival/> [accessed March 27,
2020].

34   In the UK, the war still means the Second World War, but back home, where I
come from, the war can often mean Civil. But then, sometimes I think about a writer
I know, a white man who spent his twenties warring in Afghanistan, and how once
he told me that he can no longer feel empathy for women, especially women like me.

that my faith meant a lot, but he wasn't sure he had the time or the money for further study and I wondered if I had been somewhat inconsiderate, suggesting too easily that it was worth the promise of enjoyment for a student in their late sixties to spend time and money at the institution that employs me, in part to recruit as many students as possible, without enough thought for the reality that we, my student, my institution, and I, are only just entering the thick of such unprecedented times.

Dear Heavenly Line Boats,

Do you feel sick, too, that our students are losing their livelihoods and/or lives and/or loves and we are keeping our bodies clothed and fed and sheltered with their fees?

Do you feel sick?

At some point, I think I heard you speak of the soul of our work. I think I heard you right, that you used the word soul. I wish you would tell me more about the soul of your work.

Are you both safe and well?

The email I write and send is:

March 26, 2020

Dear Heavenly Line Boats,

I hope you are staying safe. In light of the REF deadline being postponed, I would like to take some more time with my essay. Although our teaching seems to be extending well into spring break,

I am working on protecting my research time. I will be in touch with you with updates.

Best wishes,
Jodie

Yusef Komunyakaa asks, "How can love heal / the mouth shut this way?"[35] In "Safe Subjects," truth is often a disturbing force that resists comprehension:

> Redemptive as a straight razor
> against a jugular vein—
> unacknowledged & unforgiven.
> It's truth we're after here,
> hurting for, out in the streets
> where my brothers kill each other,
> each other's daughters & guardian angels
> in the opera of dead on arrival.

Toi Derricotte suggests that the uneasiness of truth stems from Komunyakaa's handling of the idea as "not a matter of conveying literal or narrative subjects." She writes:

> In fact, his earlier poems retreat from language in terms of these functions—not retreat in the sense of giving up but retreat as an act of resistance, as one retreats in military strategy. In a world where African-American identity—in particular, African-American male identity—is constantly threatened, language and the poem itself become a last defense, the ultimate weapon of the ego against dissolution. . . . For

---

35 Komunyakaa, pp. 67–68.

Komunyakaa, poetry is the expression of an embattled ego determined by whatever means necessary to survive.[36]

A heavenly line boat writes back quickly to note the postponement applies only to the administration of REF, not the dates of outputs. I should still aim to send an essay in April. The heavenly line boat notes, as well, these are difficult times, though, for sure.

I need to hit six thousand words. I seem to be especially aware of this around the stroke of midnight. 정 is a fairy tale. I reason that if I'm too tired to write but can't sleep,[37] I should go through my notes, scraps, scattered throughout my academic diary, scraps in the margins of readings for class, scraps on scraps, tangible and digital.

I find a conversation overheard on the train recorded in a draft of an email. From the date, it must have been on my last train ride into London, into Bloomsbury,[38] on to campus, where, in the summer, hundreds of tourists walk through the building where my office is,

---

36   Toi Derricotte, "The Tension Between Memory and Forgetting in the Poetry of Yusef Komunyakaa," *Kenyon Review*, New Series, 15.4 (Autumn 2003), 217–222 (p. 218).

37   When I sleep, these nights, I dream of guns: home invasions, school shootings, a muzzle tucked beneath the chin and a pale hand that is and is not mine at the trigger.

38   My love for London began in Bloomsbury, on a scholarship to study Creative Writing. I was sixteen? At some point, I cut this detail from my CV (but I still have a line, to this day, about another scholarship I won at seventeen—eighteen?—when Toni Morrison herself selected my essay about my personal hero, my mom. My English teacher that year told other students that I shouldn't have won; I was selected for optics. I wish I still had the essay, but I was seventeen or eighteen and too depressed to think to save the words I wrote, even if Toni Morrison said they mattered), but I can trace so much to being sixteen in London and spending days writing in the Bell family home.

where my classrooms are, to marvel at the dumbwaiter of the Bell family home, inside which Vanessa and Virginia are said to have played in the small and secret dark. Of course, there will be no such tourists this summer.

Why isn't Summer here?
She's waiting for us at the next stop.
Why isn't she on the train?
Because Summer doesn't live here.
When you live somewhere else, does that mean you don't use the train?
Summer doesn't use the train because she lives in the center.
The center of what?

I write six thousand words. I count the footnotes. I count words that are not mine.

Words that are not mine validate me as an academic all the time. My public-facing words: my many applications, my research profiles, all the summations of what I think I'm doing and what I want to do, language made dutiful to the interests of stakeholders. There must be a narrative of compliant individuality. I am deserving and would be most grateful if you could please let me in; I am confident that I would perform and produce to your most rightfully, most exacting standards, if only you would please let me in. There is, I think, a pale underbelly to all of us, any of us who have ever felt a kinship for those with faces who look like ours.

Don Mee Choi describes how, upon graduation from university, Kim Hyesoon worked as an editor for a publishing house during the regime of General Chun, following dictator-president Park Chung

Hee's assassination in 1979. Under Chun's regime, censorship became even more rigorous, and a play Kim Hyesoon was editing came back to her completely blackened except for the title and the writer's name.

Don Mee Choi writes:

> It is from such blackened space that, I believe, Kim Hyesoon's poetry emerges ... For Kim the blackened space is not only the space of oppression but also a place where a woman rede-fines herself, retranslates herself ... Despite South Korea's rise to relative prosperity as the world's eleventh largest economy, the degree to which it remains culturally and politi-cally subservient to the US cannot be underestimated. I need to state the obvious: South Korea is a neocolony ... Kim translates hell, as a daughter of a neocolony, and I translate her translated hell as a daughter from the neocolony—two daughters too many.[39]

Kim Hyesoon says, "I like it when a critic's hand enters my poem, touches the bone, then leaves. I like criticism that is written as though it's completing another poem upon meeting a poem in which the critic is also part of the poem."[40] In "The Way to Melodrama 4: *white day white night*," Kim Hyesoon writes:

> White snow. White rabbit. White night because white snow fell overnight. White rabbit stares at white steel-barred window. White gown. White sheet. White wrist. White hat.

---

39   DMC in KHS, pp. 158–159.

40   KHS, p. 152.

White skirt. White legs turning. White sandal. Gave birth to a white baby because of white snow. White rice that you eat while holding a white umbrella. I ate it—a white pill that makes white blood. White God inside white snow rises as high as the window. There is a white secret inside white snow. White blanket. White sweat. White skin of baby Jesus. The white wall is too high. White lips. White nose. There are too many white rats in white milk. White breath, can't breathe. There is no road because white snow keeps coming down. White devil. White hell. It's too far. White yawn. White sleep. Please untie white bandages. White writing on white paper. I will erase my white poem. Oblivious innocence of White God, open my blood's path outwards.[41]

Don Mee Choi says she was looking for a way home and found Kim Hyesoon, and I think about how Don Mee Choi, in turn, expanded home for Kim Hyesoon. This is 정 of the highest order. This is 고은정.

I stack their books and I hold their books together and I keep them close until I feel I can try to read 배수아 in Korean until I feel I can work through my fear of Theresa Hak Kyung Cha's violent, unjust death and let her words work through me. I hunger with her words, cry for mother with her words, long to return with her words, so homesick with her words that I keep out with her words, with her words line the windowsill with salt, with her words tend the ropes and the bells, with her words get through, with her words endure. Wait with her words. Wait, when I can't see the sky. Wait. I stack their books together. I hold their books close. 언니라고 불러도 될까요? I keep them close. I (un)learn and I (un)learn and I (un)learn. I have a memory of being in a public pool in Korea at the peak

---

41   KHS, p. 29.

of summer. The pool was so full of bodies that the only movement I could make was bobbing straight up and down, so that's what I did, up and down, slowly and surely, just to feel myself moving in and out of the water. I don't know how many repetitions later I broke surface to the breathless exclamation of a young man, squatting by the pool's edge to peer over at me. You're OK, he said, calm but breathless still, as if he'd been running. You know how to swim, he said. You were doing that on purpose, he said. It's only in retrospect that I think he must have been a lifeguard, that young man, younger than I am now. It's only in retrospect I think about how frightened he must have been, because in that moment what he saw was a child crowded to the deep end, slowly bobbing up and down in a classic symptom of silent drowning. But I—in the water, then—I had been completely unaware of the possibility that anyone was watching me. There were so many people in the water and so little space for me to move. I was only bobbing up and down. I remember being unable to respond to the young man, lost to my shock of being seen. I don't remember if I at least offered him a shy smile, if not a thanks, before submerging myself in the water again.

When I look back on my first two years of teaching, I think about the student who, after taking the time to ask me about how my writing was going, sat through my jumbled nervous answer, interrupting only to say, Don't do that—you're doing what you tell us not to do. Don't talk about yourself like that. .

I think about the student who, as I closed out a tutorial by asking if they had any questions, so very quietly asked, Are you happy here? Are the other lecturers nice to you?

I think about the students and staff who left for good, finding the violences unbearable. I fear my fear takes up too much space around me, in the classroom and not.

I look back on my diary from those years to try to piece together when I did what. I see handwriting that looks unrecognizable as my own. I see the way the very words on the page look deeply unwell. I think of depictions of madwomen scrawling on the walls and think, They didn't get it quite right, how it really looks, how it really feels, the words on the wall. They never do. It is day four of isolation? Time folds in on itself. I say out loud to empty rooms, 엄마, 나야, 엄마, 나 너무 힘들어.

엄마는 알지, I can hear my mother say, 엄마는 우리딸만 믿고있지.

When she was a child, my mom thought that if she ever had money, she would buy herself all the books she wanted.[42] My mom likes to talk about how her friends back in Korea knew her as the one with a way with words. I can feel my mother wanting me to believe her with some desperation because she fears I could not possibly imagine her beyond her struggle with English, beyond her struggle with America. But your daughter knows, mother. Mother, your daughter believes in you.

My mother is a gifted writer. In her late teens, as a girl from the mountains with no connections or credentials to speak of, she was hired as a bank teller in Seoul, one of the most coveted white-collar

---

42   When the day came that she started earning good money, my mother bought her mother a house and put her three younger siblings through school instead.

jobs in Korea at the time. On her first day on the job, the hiring committee informed her that she had been selected based solely on the strength of her score on the written exam. The panel had been especially moved by her essay on the importance of family.

The gift of books, my mother reserved for me. Before she and my dad bought an ice-cream store for cheap during the original owners' divorce, my mother would take me to bookstores whenever she could while my dad worked odd jobs. My mother was frugal with everything but books. I didn't always get presents for holidays or birthdays, but she always let me buy whatever book I wanted and we spent hours, hours together in bookstores while my dad did things he still doesn't talk about.

엄마는 알지.

엄마는 우리딸만 믿고있지.

An incantation I hear in my mother's voice.

We are side by side on a sofa, in a quiet corner of the bookstore. My mother is looking through architectural magazines for the pictures of American mansions. I am trying to read American poetry, wondering what "vernacular" means. In London, at Foyles in Charing Cross, I can buy Korean books. That's what I buy my mom with my first paycheck as an (almost) permanent lecturer, a(n almost) real academic. I buy my mom Korean books from London: books I'll never get to read for pleasure unless they're translated into English; translations of books I grew up reading with her by my side. My mother, she didn't have books growing up. My mother's mother had too many daughters and so sent one, my mother, to live with her mother in the mountains. I often feel from my mother that it was not a kind life. I often feel my mother should have been entitled to a life more like mine.[43]

When my mother was two, she was pronounced dead. She was still with her mother then, but it was a time and a place when a fever could kill. My mother had stopped breathing by the time the village medicine man arrived. My grandmother washed my mother's body with well water and wrapped her in undyed linen. All the while, my grandmother thought mostly of a son who had been stillborn and how perhaps her ancestors had cursed her womb. She prepared three bowls of white rice and poured three cups of well water. She set a small, low table by my mother's body, thought again of the son lost to her before my mother, and went to sleep.

That night, my grandmother dreamt of three old women in white gliding into her home. They sat around the small, low table, the full skirts of their 한복 arranged carefully around them. "It's been so long since we've been offered a meal," one of the women, the one with the whitest hair, said, gently-gently picking up a silver spoon from the small and low table. She took the first bite of rice and the two other women followed suit. They took their time. They emptied their bowls. Then they drank their water, every last drop. Then the three women stilled before turning slowly toward my mother's shrouded

---

43   This is the fairy-tale ending: A life rich with books and a deep love for words, working with books and words and people who, even with flawed and broken means, push and push for there to be more books and more words in this world. We are not the right kind of doctors, no, not at this pivotal moment in time. But I could always feel how proud my mother was of me when I was reading. I can feel how proud she is of me for writing. I can feel it in every good word I write.

body, which began to glow with such light that my grandmother was startled awake.

It was not yet dawn when my grandmother rushed to unwrap my mother's shroud. Inside, my mother's forehead was beaded with sweat and her mouth was agape with the noisy breath of a deep, exhausted sleep.[44]

I wonder if awe is why my mother's mother sent her away to the mountains, to her own mother, to be raised as such a distant daughter that when my mother came to America and reunited with her youngest sister, the aunt who beat me, she told my mother, I never thought of you as a sister. I always thought you were adopted, or some poor, distant cousin who needed our charity. And that's why you tried so hard to be a part of the family. That's why you tried so hard to be like another mother to us.[45]

Theresa 학경 Cha, who wrote a book, *FOR HER MOTHER FOR HER FATHER*, writes in *Dictee*:

어머니 you who take the child from your back to your breast you who unbare your breast to the child her hunger is your own the child takes away your pain with her nourishment

어머니 you who take the husband from your back to your breast you who unbare your breast to the husband his hun-

---

44 My mother has told me this story three times. Each time, it changes slightly. It could be her memory or mine, her translation or mine. It could be Korean or English.

45 I wish my mother and I could exorcise her.

ger your own the husband takes away your pain with his
nourishment[46]

I don't call my mother as often as I dream of her. In my dreams, I tell
my mother I love her, rushing to try to tell her how much because
I know I will wake up soon. Sometimes the dreams are too sad
and the rooms of my childhood home I float through are dark and
empty. Do you dream of me, mother? 엄마, I want go home. 엄마, I
want to climb yonder up high.

Can you see her on the mountain? She is my mother there, on the
precipice, and she is me, too, the woman in white. Her hair, our hair,
is long and loose and unseemly. Our hair is dark, you know this
well, the well we climb out of, that hell we are bound to by the power
of some kind of wrong done unto us. You've been told we are always
angry. You've been told we will come for you from the deep water,
from anywhere that is as dark as our hair. My mother and I, we open
our mouth, our mouth that is ours.[47] Inside, there are no teeth, only
a deeper dark and the faintly sweet smell of rot. You do not like the
smell, we know, we can tell by the way you shiver when you ask, But
what about the bad words?[48]

When we wail, it is very, very different from how I told you it would
be. When we wail, it is not a sound that can be written down. Well,
well, I can only tell you that there are no words.

---

46   Theresa 학경 Cha, *Dictee* (University of California Press, 2001), p. 109. "Mother"
from the original text has been translated into Korean here.

47   You must know it is ours, our mouth.

48   You may cover your ears now.

[Water Damage, Dates Unknown]

Dear Manchester Chinatown,

I lived down the street from your gates during 2010–2015. I was in my twenties, an international student living on my own for the first time, in a studio flat smaller than my childhood bedroom. My building was behind an art gallery, next to a casino, which was across the street from a strip club.

You were loud.

And lit up on nights I walked home alone. You were the pocket of a foreign city where I could breathe easier among faces that looked more like mine.

You have to understand that for some of those years, I was still trying to tell myself that finding comfort among faces that looked like mine shouldn't matter, that maybe it was even wrong of me to feel this way. You saw me through a master's, and then my doctorate. Apart from ending up in your neighborhood, largely by chance but also by circumstance, I was continuing a trajectory of being surrounded by many white and well-to-do faces.

In those years, Barack Hussein Obama was my president. I was trying to keep quiet about why it pained me to hear white Americans talk about how nice Black people were to them when they wore his campaign paraphernalia in public, and the #joy they found in this being extended overseas, how nice all people Black and Brown could be at the sight of an Obama shirt. I didn't know what to make of the many mouth sounds that came from highly educated and wealthy white people who sincerely felt that keeping a bumper sticker on their car or a button on their backpack was hard proof of having solved the issue of race, or that it had never really existed at all, America's race problem; I didn't know where to start.

I was still trying to swallow back why I didn't want white people to talk at me about their activism and allyship but really about Black people. Specifically, I didn't want white people to talk at me about Black people in ways that felt conspiratorial, one-sided conversations that relentlessly led to claims of not seeing color, but especially not seeing color when it came to people like me. I felt amorphous, water to be tested.

I have noticed a tendency in white people to take photos of me with my eyes closed. That is to say, they will pick and choose and disseminate photos of me with my eyes closed while they would never knowingly do so to a white subject. In group photos with white people, I am the only one with my eyes closed. I often cannot bear to look at photos of myself taken by white friends, taken by white family.

This is what I must look like to them at all times: my eyes are always closed.

I sometimes wonder how much it frightens them to look into the black of my eyes.

David L. Eng and Shinhee Han write in *Racial Melancholia, Racial Dissociation: On the Social and Psychic Lives of Asian Americans* (2019):

> Over a hundred years ago, W. E. B. Du Bois asked African Americans in *The Souls of Black Folk* (1903), "How does it feel to be a problem?" Today, comparative race scholars have

revised Du Bois's earlier inquiry, asking Asian Americans, "How does it feel to be a solution?" Put in terms of comparative race relations, Ellen Wu observes that during the prewar era of exclusion and yellow peril, Asians were defined as definitely not white. However, following the postwar era of inclusion, citizenship, and the emergence of model minority stereotype, Asians were defined as definitely not black. Understanding this triangulation is key to apprehending the ways in which racial binaries of black and white mask complex social relations of race while preventing political coalitions and alliances. Effacing unequal histories of racial discrimination, this divide and conquer strategy emerges most forcefully today in contemporary debates about affirmative action that seek to pit the interests of African Americans and Asian Americans against one another.

For too many of those years I lived in your neighborhood, I still longed to be a good immigrant, the best kind of American I could be. I wanted to write about home, in part to prove that America was my home, specifically the American South where I grew up.

They named my neighborhood Providence. Over farmland that itself was worked brutally over swamp that used to cover nearly everything, they built a white-peaked country club like a wedding cake and rolled out a golf course all around it. Once, an old white president with a penchant for sexually assaulting young women visited the links. This is a point of pride.

In the hours before the second presidential debate of 2016, the orange monster broadcast himself live through Facebook, flanked by Juanita Broaddrick, Paula Jones, and Kathleen Willey, three women who wanted to speak out against Bill Clinton, and Kathy

Shelton, whose rapist had been defended by Hillary Clinton in court. Shelton was twelve years old when she was raped by a forty-one-year-old man. Hillary Clinton's court-ordered defense enabled the rapist to plead to a lesser charge.

Juanita Broaddrick said, "Actions speak louder than words. Mr. Trump may have said some bad words, but Bill Clinton raped me and Hillary Clinton threatened me. I don't think there's anything worse." I could taste fluorescent green rising at the back of my throat, like chewed tender grass. My mother likes to remind me that we are both rabbits in the zodiac. I wonder if it is a kind of power, the way we feel terror in premonition, in a way we know must be inherited somehow, this other sense that raises our hairs, holds our bodies taut and tense and so still, you must know what I mean, our ability to know with absolute certainty we are in grave danger.

The houses of Providence, like its country club, replicate proud old colonials, with expansive lawns that puddle deep with rain. You could build a pool, a landscaper suggested once. When I translated this to my mother, she expelled a bitter laugh through her nose, wondering who would waste money like that and knowing exactly who. The handful of friends I had in the neighborhood all had a pool and/or a trampoline. I learned to be especially cautious around pools and/or trampolines from the number of times a white mother singled me out to tell me to get out of her pool or off her trampoline, as she didn't know who my parents were. Imagine, the white mother said, if I injured myself on her property and my parents sued her. This happened three times, which some may say is not that many. Through manicured streets designed to tastefully evoke winding country roads, I rode bikes with children of bankers, lawyers, doctors, and professors whose parents always asked me where exactly my parents and I lived in the neighborhood, what street, which house, exactly.

I learned how to drive on those same streets. I didn't understand why my dad insisted that I practice in my mom's only slightly old Mercedes instead of his ancient minivan. I thought maybe it was another hard lesson in working well under pressure, gritting our teeth to keep sight of aspirations, exactly what a crazy, uptight Asian parent would do, until a cop on regular patrol of our neighborhood started trailing us. We hadn't made it far beyond our driveway, but my dad directed me back as he opened our garage door. When the cop saw that, he smiled, waved at us, and drove on. There are many signs throughout the neighborhood I grew up in declaring in blue on white: OFFICERS ON PATROL HERE.

I obviously am not white-passing, but I continue to have access to many white-passing privileges, such as the police not inexplicably and brutally murdering me or my father. You understand, the price of my privilege wasn't always something I had to think about, unless I really needed or wanted to.

That driving lesson is one of the few intact memories I have of spending time alone with my dad as a kid. I remember him best as the passing smell of sugar and butterfat. Unlike the parents of the white children in my neighborhood, my parents owned and operated an ice-cream store, still do, though that's harder to say definitively now, isn't it? I don't know what will become of small businesses in the years to come. Are you staying safe and well?

On your crowded sidewalks, I'd fall into rhythm just a step or two behind a tiny older woman slumped in the shoulders. I'd stare at her short, curly hair showing gray at the roots and imagine I was walking with my mom. I'd pass men chain-smoking in your dark alleyways with an apron over the shoulder or a dishrag still in hand, and better understand my dad, who was hardly ever home.

When drunk white men spilling out of cocktail bars would shout knee how at me, I knew they wouldn't dare approach me in your neighborhood, among my people.

"Your people" is what an artist manning an installation piece on Manchester's campus said to me. The installation was a large cage of books and it was making a statement about subversion and accessibility of knowledge. People were meant to walk around and browse within the cage, but the artist stopped me and said, "You can read this one."

I was startled by the way he thrust the book at me with one hand, arm extended in full, expecting me to close in on the distance between us to reach it. I apologized and explained that I can't read Chinese. He didn't quite believe me. "But this is your people," he said.

As a teaching assistant, in rooms full of white faces, I laughed along to the open mockery of essays written by Chinese international students in marking meetings, a tactic seemingly deployed by established academics to encourage camaraderie with graduate students who weren't getting paid for marking. I felt eyes on me whenever the word "Chinese" came up. The term "cash cow" was one I heard often, but it was never overtly directed at me.

I have many painful memories of English as a second language: in Korea, my kindergarten origami instructor teaching us the word "A-F-R-I-C-A," just so she could tell us not to fold our precious colored paper messily, as Africans would; in America, being the only one called out of my high school English class under orders of the No Child Left Behind Act, missing a lesson on Romeo and Juliet to take a standardized test with standardized tasks such as writing a brief sentence surmising the scene of a family enjoying a picnic, a mother, a father, a son, and daughter, all smiling and white. I remember starting to write something angry before erasing it. I remember writing instead about the bond of family.

There was a time when what I thought I really needed and wanted was to feel a greater sense of legitimacy. I thought studying in the UK, home of so many writers I was taught to admire, would better me as a writer with more distance and perspective, ultimately making me a better immigrant, a better American. There was a time I wanted this very badly. In the UK, whenever who and what I was and where exactly I came from were met with a kind of lurid fascination and an unwavering conviction that race was distinctly an American problem, I often relented.

Maybe that's why in the UK I felt more drawn than ever to writing my way into acts of violence that felt historied and unending, in the very air we breathe, without fully contending with why. It was in the UK that I started turning away from the English canon staked for so long into my heart and wondered if I could better identify with the Southern Gothic.

Born in the small town of Bogalusa, Louisiana, as James William Brown, Yusef Komunyakaa, grew up during the time of the civil rights movement, eventually taking on the name of his grandfather, a stowaway to America from Trinidad. There is a classic Gothic quality to the very creation of *Neon Vernacular* (1993), in which Komunyakaa boldly stitched together a collection of twelve new poems with selections from his seven earlier volumes of poetry. The tome gave new life to the career of the once–poet's poet, winning the Pulitzer Prize in 1994. In curating his own oeuvre under the declaration of a new language, Komunyakaa provokes participation in the living dialogue of his poetry, urging acts of transcription, transposition, and translation. We are led to transgression, acts of defiance.

In his poem "Audacity of the Lower Gods," Komunyakaa writes:

> I know salt marshes that move along like one big
> trembling wing. I've noticed insects
> shiny as gold in a blues singer's teeth
> & more keenly calibrated than a railroad watch,
> but at heart I'm another breed.

Can you feel the longing for home alongside the terrible sense of displacement here, the yearning of a creature to belong to the land—not man, but breed—beyond the realms of both the natural and the industrial worlds, its heart neither organic nor man-made. I know you know this is not really a question.

Ruminating on the abject horror of the Middle Passage, Leila Taylor writes in *Darkly: Black History and America's Gothic Soul* (2019), "Blackness in America is still in the middle, residing in the place between opposites: living in the present while carrying the past, being human but perceived as other, considered both a person and a product, both American and foreign, neither here nor there."

On February 26, 2012, Trayvon Martin was murdered. A nearly all-white jury acquitted Trayvon's murderer on July 13, 2013. Reporting for the *Washington Post*, Janell Ross credits three women for igniting the Black Lives Matter movement in the hours following the verdict: Alicia Garza, Patrisse Cullors, and Opal Tometi.

Trayvon Martin was seventeen years old. Trayvon had dreams of flying. In *Rest in Power: The Enduring Life of Trayvon Martin* (2017),

Trayvon's mother, Sybrina Fulton, writes of a day Trayvon came home from aviation camp:

> One day at the camp, Trayvon sat in the cockpit of Barrington Irving's globe-trotting airplane. When he came home, he still had stars in his eyes. "Mom, I know what I'm going to do," he told me. He had decided on a career in aviation: either as a mechanic (because he could fix *anything*) or as a professional pilot. He couldn't decide which, except that he was determined to *be around planes.*

I think about how the use of italics alongside and apart from direct quotes conveys the sense that Trayvon's mom must feel his voice, feel his words, with her, still, in ways that we cannot fully understand.

In *Citizen: An American Lyric*, Claudia Rankine speaks:

> If I called I'd say good-bye before I broke the good-bye. I say good-bye before anyone can hang up. Don't hang up. My brother hangs up though he is there. I keep talking. The talk keeps him there. The sky is blue, kind of blue. The day is hot. Is it cold? Are you cold? It does get cool. Is it cool? Are you cool?
>
> My brother is completed by the sky. The sky is his silence. Eventually, he says, it is raining. It is raining down. It was raining. It stopped raining. It is raining down. He won't hang up. He's there, he's there but he's hung up though he is there. Good-bye, I say. I break the good-bye. I say good-bye before anyone can hang up, don't hang up. Wait with me. Wait with me though the waiting might be the call of good-byes.

Over eight years since Trayvon was murdered, I'm still hearing highly educated and wealthy white people retort that all lives matter, worse still that blue lives matter. Blue on white on white on white unending; my jaw has been clenched against it for so long.

I was warned of Manchester rain, but not of the way faces like mine meant we all became Chinese. When I registered with the local GP, the nearest to me and yet beyond your territory, I was called in for a health check that consisted of the nurse asking me why I hadn't ticked a box to declare my race. She said, "You can pick Chinese or Asian (Other)."

"I'm not sure," I said, apologetic.

"You have to pick one," she said. "Chinese?"

My first medical appointment there was for a UTI. The doctor who saw me sat much too close to say, "So you've moved here and now you're having too much sex." I think I laughed nervously and/or looked off into some unfixed distance, as I do. I remember he looked and sounded like Santa Claus with received pronunciation. I remember his eyes fast lost his twinkle, his mirth, his ho ho ho, replaced by something sharper. He didn't quite believe my utterly American English, my calm explanation that the women in my family have a history of UTIs and that the stress of living in a new city alone was likely causing mine. The doctor looked down at my file and studied it for some time, "Ah, the American South," he said. "Home of stunning antebellum mansions."

There was a particularly brutal Ph.D. workshop when I was told by a white woman to watch *Gone With the Wind* to better visualize the American South, that when she thought of the Civil War, what she saw were those gorgeous dresses the belles wore. There weren't any such dresses in the chapter she'd read of my novel, and that really disappointed her. I remained silent for the duration of my portion of the workshop, keeping my head down to take notes, listening to one white woman after the other, a white man leading the circle, nodding his approval.

Before and during the Civil War, white writers from all across America and beyond wrote in defense of slavery. After the American Civil War, white writers from all across America and beyond began to write with nostalgia for slavery, or, academically put, an idealization of antebellum society, glorifying the Confederacy and mourning the Golden Era lost to them. This hasn't stopped. Black literature continues to stand in defiance of the prioritizing of white feelings and white experiences central to a linear reading of the conventional history of the Southern Gothic.

Charles W. Chesnutt's voice as a Black man who could have passed as white but chose not to do so brings a complexity to his work that resists resolution. The subversive social commentary in Chesnutt's most famous work, *The Conjure Woman* (1899), has only relatively recently been studied with greater gravity, to position Chesnutt as one of the most significant American writers of the late nineteenth and early twentieth centuries.

In "The Goophered Grapevine," a white northerner meets Uncle Julius, introducing readers to the central character of *The Conjure Woman* with the unflinching racism more commonly attributed to southerners:

> He resumed his seat with somewhat of embarrassment.
> While he had been standing, I had observed that he was a

tall man, and, though slightly bowed by the weight of years, apparently quite vigorous. He was not entirely black, and this fact, together with the quality of his hair, which was about six inches long and very bushy, except on the top of his head, where he was quite bald, suggested a slight strain of other than negro blood. There was a shrewdness in his eyes, too, which was not altogether African, and which, as we afterwards learned from experience, was indicative of a corresponding shrewdness in his character.

Unlike the typical fervent poetics of a white southerner describing a Black man, the tone of the white northerner has a sense of clinical observation. The "quality" of Julius's hair and the "shrewdness" of his eyes speak to the whiteness that is the "slight strain of other" that ultimately makes Julius unsettling to the white northerner, because whiteness fears to be recognized for what it is. We know the "somewhat of embarrassment" is a presumption made by the white northerner as first-person perspective limits such knowledge, particularly for a narrator so clearly lacking in empathy, speaking more to the need for the white northerner's shame. Chesnutt imbues whiteness with a viral, disease-like quality, suggesting that the quality and arrogance of whiteness fully embodied in the alien presence of the white northerner yet only a strain in Julius, is an infectious threat to the Black man.

As the nameless white northerner notes that Julius is a tall man "though slightly bowed by the weight of years," Chesnutt signals for the reader the significance of Julius's role in *The Conjure Woman* in two ways: that there is literally more to Julius's stature than meets the eye; that there will be a name and a complex history to the Black man, while the abstracted white northerner remains unnamed. By introducing readers to Uncle Julius through a northern white man's eyes, Chesnutt calls for an upheaval of the discourse on race, you know, in 1899.

On June 17, 2015, nine parishioners of Emanuel African Methodist Episcopal Church in Charleston, South Carolina, were shot and killed by a white man who had been welcomed to their late-night Bible study session. The nine victims are: Reverent Clementa C. Pinckney, Reverend Sharonda Coleman-Singleton, Reverend DePayne Middleton-Doctor, Reverend Daniel Simmons Sr., Cynthia Hurd, Ethel Lance, Myra Thompson, Susie Jackson, and Tywanza Sanders.

A statement from the Africana Studies and Research Center at Cornell University explains the significance of Mother Emanuel:

> The Emanuel AME church has a stellar history of resistance and spiritual nurturing that began with its founding in 1816 by enslaved and free blacks and, together with other such places of worship in the country, became a beacon of inspiration to African Americans in their calls for justice, equality, and moral reckoning for generations. This history in which resistance to injustice and the nurturing of the faithful are inextricably intertwined helps to explain why the church's faithful refer to it as Mother Emanuel. We are saddened and enraged that the faithful were killed after extending hospitality to a stranger in this most sacred and historically important place of black leadership in the United States.

Eleven days after the mass murder at Mother Emanuel, I came across a *Vogue* spread on a Southern Gothic dream wedding, a collage of images featuring waifish white women in bridal lace and luxury accessories ringing the central image of the Huguenot Church in

Charleston, South Carolina, labeled with the words, "The Holy City." The feature was described as "a love letter to [. . .] Charleston" by the editor who created it, who calls Charleston her hometown.

Not a month after the mass murder at Mother Emanuel, on the day of American Independence, the *Guardian* ran an essay by a white man entitled "Why Southern Gothic Rules the World," in which the author reminds his readers that the Civil War is long gone and that people living in the American South today did not personally create the problems faced by the American South.

The loss of these nine Black lives at Mother Emanuel prompted intensified protests against the Confederate flag flown prominently atop a dome of the South Carolina Statehouse since the 1960s, when it was placed to commemorate the Civil War centennial as a symbol of the state's defiance of integration and the civil rights movement. This one flag was successfully removed on July 9, 2015.

A day after the hate crime at Mother Emanuel, the *New York Times* published an online curation of six attacks on Black churches starting with the burning of a church in Springfield, Massachusetts, by three white men shortly after the election of President Obama in 2008, tracing back to the Ku Klux Klan's 1963 bombing of Sixteenth Street Church in Birmingham, Alabama. In the week following the hate crime at Mother Emanuel, at least five Black southern churches were set on fire.

On September 15, 1963, Addie Mae Collins, Cynthia Wesley, Carole Robertson, all age fourteen, and Denise McNair, age eleven, were murdered when the KKK planted approximately fifteen sticks of dynamite under the steps of Sixteenth Street Church. More than twenty other members of the congregation were injured. The hate crime at Sixteenth Street Church is cited as a major catalyst for the civil rights movement and the eventual passage of the Civil Rights Act of 1964. Although the FBI and local authorities had four strong suspects, no prosecutions were made until 1977, when just one of the original suspects was convicted for the murder of Denise McNair alone. It took until 2002 to convict two more of the original suspects. The fourth remaining suspect had died in 1994.

At the age of twenty-six, Tywanza Kibwe Diop Sanders was the youngest victim of the hate crime at Mother Emanuel. Tywanza died while trying to reason with the gunman while shielding his great-aunt, Susie Jackson, with his body. Susie Jackson, age eighty-seven, was the oldest victim of the massacre.

When the hate crime at Mother Emanuel occurred, I had three months left to finish my doctoral thesis. In my thesis, most of the victims' names, victims of the mass murder at Mother Emanuel and of the mass murder at Sixteenth Street Church, were in the footnotes.

Who am I to lecture you?

Who do I think I am?

Novelist, poet, and historical sociologist Erna Brodber's novel *Louisiana* (1994) opens with a fictional editor's notes on the text, harking back to the letters of authenticity accompanying the literary hoax of *Otranto*. Brodber's false preface explains that the text we are about to read includes transcripts of tape recordings from an academic's failed case study on Black life in Louisiana.

As Jamaican Brodber imagines African American Ella Townsend's conversations with spirits transcribed onto the page from audio recordings, her prose departs to the realm of poetry, singing of the significance of translation as an act of shifting from life to other realms:

> And they were all there. Every jack one of them I had told you about was there to celebrate my translation. They came in carts and every scrammie there was; they came through short cuts with their shoes in their hands; up shalley hillsides with nothing but coconut oil on their feet. They came in groups; they came alone. They came with [. . .] their velvet banners in the brightest reds and blues, the words embossed in opposite colours, tassels flying; they came in long white gloves; they came with swords; Ezekiel's boom-boom band with the round white faced drum, pulling itself up the hillside by sheer faith.
>
> White is the funeral colour here as there. Against the green of the trees, the black of their skins, the vibrant colours of their banners, it telescoped one loud clear report, "Hail Aunt Louise," I could cry. Anna, I was seeing every corner of that scene. Being translated is like that. You can see from every angle. And I tell you. What a sight! Like so many clean white birds nestling in a Portland thicket [. . .] shaded by the flowering mulatto companion tree. And the singing. Vox populi. *I hear the voice, the gentle voice. Is the voice of God. That calls me home.*

Here, the funeral is translated as a celebration of life, lending itself to loud, painterly colors. Particularly resonant is the joyous reclamation of the color white, of its purity and sanctity to Black culture. Brodber's transcendent prose poetry gives room for this celebration of translation to resound across place and time, history and fiction, the author's lived experience, memory, and imaginings as well as those of Ella Townsend's, both author and character enacting so many identities, urging the reader to participate in the intersection of it all, a plenitude of everything happening at once, in this life and elsewhere, wherever that may be.

Brodber's generous literature is invested in the idea of unity through differences. Born in Jamaica in 1940, Brodber states a primary concern of her work in an interview from 2002:

> I believe it is necessary to the development of black people and therefore the development of the world if black people get together. There are large fissures between African Americans and African Caribbean people that need to be bridged.

In the *Journal of West Indian Literature* (April 2005), writer and academic Kezia Page adds to this that:

> Brodber's *Louisiana*, consistent with the spirit of a novel concerned with making connections, explores trans-cultural alliances as important psychic and cultural progress for black people, but even more so, because *Louisiana* is set in the 1930s, in the USA, in the South.

Do you think homesickness kills?

I was warned by friends and family claiming intimacy with London, Cambridge, and/or Oxford, that Manchester is a rough city. I was warned of rival gangs—rival Chinese gangs, it was always qualified—fighting for your turf, of stabbings in broad daylight on your busy streets. But no one warned me that when riding a bus in London, I shouldn't try to pay by holding the money out with both hands, a gesture ingrained in me since my birth in Korea, the passing of something with both of your hands into someone else's hands, always with both hands to show the other person: I have this much care for you.

"Put the fucking money on the fucking tray," the bus driver said. "Fucking Chinese."

In the days before the first wave of lockdown began, I was walking across one of the squares around my office in Bloomsbury—I still don't know which is which, to be honest with you—when I was struck by the way a man I'd never seen before was staring at me. I know I don't have to tell you that it really did feel something like being struck, a blow to some softer part of us. I know I don't have to tell you that he was white. I know I don't have to tell you that his eyes were filled with a kind of hate I recognized innately. In his eyes, I was the virus. I thought of you then, and wondered if it's better where you are. You don't have to tell me that it isn't; we know, you and I.

In Randall Kenan's "The Foundations of the Earth," from *Let the Dead Bury Their Dead* (1992), Mrs. Maggie MacGown Williams looks out from her porch, wishing she was alone:

> And fields surrounded Mrs. Maggie MacGowan Williams's house, giving the impression that her lawn stretched on and on until it dropped off into the woods far by the way. Sometimes she was certain she could actually see the earth's curve—not merely the bend of the small hill on which her house sat but the great slope of the sphere, the way scientists explained it in books, a monstrous globe floating in a cold nothingness. She would sometimes sit by herself on the patio late of an evening, in the same chair she was sitting in now, sip from her Coca-Cola, and think about how big the earth must be to seem flat to the eye.

At once ringed by people and a "monstrous globe floating in a cold nothingness," Mrs. Maggie MacGowan Williams is suffering from the symptoms of her speculative cosmology. Meanwhile, Kenan's prose sings, calling for a revolution, a new world order.

In *Go Tell It on the Mountain* (1953), James Baldwin writes:

> "Run on, little brother," Elisha said. "Don't you get weary. God won't forget you. You won't forget."
>
> Then he turned away, down the long avenue, home. John stood still, watching him walk away. The sun had come full awake. It was waking the streets and the houses, and crying at the windows. It fell over Elisha like a golden robe, and struck John's forehead, where Elisha had kissed him, like a seal ineffaceable forever.
>
> And he felt his father behind him. And he felt the March wind rise, striking through his damp clothes, against his salty body. He turned to face his father—he found himself smiling, but his father did not smile.
>
> They looked at each other a moment. His mother stood in the doorway, in the long shadows of the hall.
>
> "I'm ready," John said, "I'm coming. I'm on my way."

In America, I lived in quieter, greener spaces with songbirds in the morning and crickets at night. But you became my town. In your restaurants, all I ever had to do was order and pay for my food. I learned to ask for char siu, which was more streamlined than asking for pork on rice. I learned that I could ask for my choice combination of vegetables in oyster sauce, off-menu (straw mushrooms, baby sweetcorn, and bamboo shoots). You packed my takeaway carton so full, the lid would barely close.

Once, when I came back to rainy Manchester after a long visit with my parents, the owner of Happy Seasons recognized my order and said, "You haven't called in a while." I felt then what I felt going to the one Korean restaurant on your outskirts, when I could speak in my broken Korean to the young owner and call her 언니 and hear her call the older women in the kitchen 이모, both of these words which sound a little like 엄마.

I rarely speak Korean with anyone but my parents—I'm too self-conscious of how broken it is—but I was caught off guard by 언니's delight when I paid for my meal with both hands.

"어머!" she said, which sounds a little like 언니 and 이모 and 엄마. She smiled and held out my change with both of her hands. "You're Korean," she said.

"네," I said, grateful and proud.

I got my Ph.D. in the end. I have a job that I love enough to try to be motivated by perpetual imposter syndrome rather than debilitated by it.

I owe a tremendous debt to Black literature, Black scholarship, and Black activism, to Black lives lived more generously than mine. It is a debt that I cannot repay in this lifetime, but I am trying my best to honor it and give in kind as a writer and educator.

My position is secure enough that I hardly ever hear the *d*-word to my face: diversity hire. I will do everything in my power to ensure there are more faces like mine in academia, more people of color, but most importantly, more Black scholars in secure, permanent posts. I will do everything in my power to ensure our progress is marked, if slow and painful and unending. But you know, don't you, with your lights and your loud and your scents of longing, that I am often scared and sad and lonely in a way I cannot fully contend with if I want to keep breathing.

Reni Eddo-Lodge writes in *Why I'm No Longer Talking to White People About Race* (Bloomsbury, 2017):

> Change is incremental, and racism will exist long after I die. But if you're committed to anti-racism, you're in it for the long haul. It will be difficult. Getting to the end point will require you to be uncomfortable.

Komunyakaa's "Epilogue to the Opera of Dead on Arrival" opens with what could be such a hopeful line:

> I can still sing
> "Ain't Going Down to the Well
> No Mo'" like Leadbelly.
> Blow out the candles
> & start anew.

But the song that could be sung is a work holler about tests of faith. And even if it could be sung, it would be in pale imitation of Leadbelly, patron saint of the blues. Without due invocation, without the presence of true song, the absence of the repeated lines "I ain't going down / I ain't going down / Oh I ain't going down to the well no mo'" resounds as a futile resistance of being sunk so low, a desperate denial of sin rather than a resolution to stand tall. We already know that a childish wish with a single breath will never be sated. As the candles blow out, in the darkness we are taken back to a lovers' tomb. But the story here is all wrong. The roles are reversed. Juliet shouldn't be dead first. That is, that woman shouldn't be dead like that. The speaker, that is, Romeo, he shouldn't be touching her like that.

> Where's Sweet Luck? —
> a kiss from that woman.
> It's the way starlight
> struck the blade. If only
> I could push down on her chest
> & blow a little breath
> into her mouth, maybe.

He should have saved that single breath for her, maybe. But it's not so much the story's changed, only that it's already ended. It's only that the lovers are already dead, have been dead for some time. Romeo, that is, the speaker, isn't touching her at all, much less blowing her like a horn. Or was it candles? Or maybe I'm getting confused because I missed that lesson on *Romeo and Juliet*.

Even in spirit, he is denied her body and soul. Only he has returned to their cold grave. In this hollowed-out ground, there is something like Prayer of Prayers, an inhalation, if you will, toward the end of the epilogue, an extension of that last breath wish:

> Handcuff me, slam my head
> against bars of the jailhouse,
> use your blackjacks,
> zero in on my weaknesses,
> let enough melancholy
> to kill a mule
> settle into my lungs.

But it's all useless here. No more crime or punishment. Only the echo of Leadbelly again, that old outlaw, that Black murderer. We don't need deep love or deep violence to silence us anymore. It's all there is, this strange little verse that is a scrap of silence. There's no more ending to wish for, no more love or luck, there is no song. There's not enough air for any more breath, much less sound. We can wait, but it won't come back. She won't come back. We were warned about this opera from the start. We were warned about the stage, all the men and women. This is the end of the line.

There's a retirement speech from a very famous white male professor that other white people have probably described a lot as luminous. Full disclosure, this particular very famous white male professor happened to be retiring from the university I earned my bachelor's from, the same university Professor Randall Kenan earned his bachelor's from and now teaches at. In this retirement speech, the very famous white male professor contends, entirely with good intention, that there is a single, simple test for the quality of southernness in literature: Is there a dead mule in it?

While the very famous white male professor largely makes light of what he describes as the Dead Mule Zone, referred throughout his speech as DMZ, Komunyakaa spends the last scraps of his "Epilogue" resisting the white space of a blank page—the silence there—on an Imagined Mule Death (IMD) instead.

Mules, in white southern literature, are often viewed with the pity appropriately reserved for poor beasts. At the same time, the ire against them is often justified by the idea that these dumb animals should be grateful for being fed and sheltered to do no more than work the land, that as much love and kindness and good intentions their owners can give them, these ill-natured creatures are bound to turn nasty. On September 22, 1862, the Day of Jubilee, a proposal set forth by northern politicians for the Reconstruction was to give every former slave land and a mule. After all, Black hands had worked the stubborn, obstinate, foul-tempered beasts best all this time.

In "Epilogue to the Opera of Dead on Arrival," the dying wish of the speaker is that we take what moment we have left to us to find empathy for the poor mule, the black and ugly spirit animal of St. Leadbelly of the Blues. We can look into that white space and know there are mass graves of bodies that when living were considered no better than beasts.

I think of Flannery O'Connor's letter responding to Maryat Lee's suggestion that James Baldwin could visit her while he was in Georgia, how O'Connor wrote, "Might as well expect a mule to fly as me to see James Baldwin in Georgia."

O'Connor writes:

> No I can't see James Baldwin in Georgia. It would cause the greatest trouble and disturbance and disunion. In New York it would be nice to meet him; here it would not. I observe the traditions of the society I feed on—it's only fair.

I think of the very famous white male professor's speech and recall, too, the way the letters DMZ felt cutting on the page; I think of the country I was born in and the DMZ that further wounds the first land I called home; I think of the women who gave language to me and I (un)learn: "I remain a daughter of neocolony."

Don Mee Choi further writes in *DMZ Colony* (2020):

I'll leave it up to your imagination what a DMZ village looks like, what his house looks like, what his dogs look like, how many of his teeth are missing, how fit he still is, how he carefully peels sweet potatoes roasted in his woodstove, how terribly beautiful the Han River looks behind the endless barbed-wire fence, how many soldiers guard the Civilian Control Zone, how he points to the river, how the river connects to the Imjin River, flowing from the north to south, what a country that's not a country looks like, what smoke that's not smoke looks like, how he tilts his gaze sideways when he says I'll leave it up to your imagination, the size of the blisters, whether a political view can be changed or not, whether a divided country is a country or not, what shock sounds like, how this really was the world, how deep the well was, whether the acacia tree was in bloom or not.

Somewhere, on the other side, are still-loved-ones. Somewhere, on the other side, is a woman who may share the blood of my father and/or my mother, a woman who houses many spirits inside her, shameful and shunned and only ever whispered of again. I don't know how much, if any, is memory from what my mother told me, how much, if any, is memory from overhearing the women who survived of my mother's family back when I was a child in Seoul, I don't know if I imagined it, this memory of my mother jabbing me so sharply in the side with her finger when I asked my father, "아빠, 아빠가족에 무당 있어?" and I would ask "무당 있어? 있어? 있어?" and persist until distracted by something sweet or something else or just because outside the window I could see light dance in the trees, but I think I know that particular memory, not the dream, but the memory as it happened, with an uncle, not my father who was never home, at the wheel, the green and gold and the slow, smothering heat—that dark that began to open up beneath me, gently-gently, took place inside a car. I don't know how much I am making up. I don't mean to tell lies. I am always trying to remember, and not.

It will be 2021 when I learn that my mother's mother had a scar on her forehead from being struck by a Japanese police officer during the occupation. My mother lingers on the way her mother lingered on the way so much blood ran down her face she feared she would breathe it in, her own blood, and choke on it. My mother says her mother didn't want to tell her much more than that.

My father counts the years. He asks my mother if it was '44 or '45. My mother says it was the year her mother birthed then lost her son. My father says it feels like Korea has forgotten how starved it used to be and I think he might tell me something of his childhood, but he doesn't, and I think about how, in these other lands I've come to call home sometimes, when their people are scared, they tend to cry for god, but I come from a place where we cry for our mothers— 엄마야! 엄마! 엄마! My mother tells stories in my father's stead, how starved she was and how she longed for meat. There was never any meat in my mother's mother's house, my mother says, so I could only taste it on feast days, when a rich house would share with the village, sometimes.

Dear Manchester Chinatown, you were at your most generous on Chinese New Year, what I have always known as Lunar New Year. I remember you—louder and brighter than ever—red and gold and grease, sugar and salt and families. In this way, I often imagined a life had I been raised in communities with faces more like mine, celebrating the passing of time marked by the moon, breathing in the gunpowder of fireworks, cooking our many rich foods, speaking our many loud tongues which are supposedly always louder than English of any kind.

I thought of you because you sheltered me and fed me better than England alone ever could. I thought of you because I miss feeling somewhat at home with you. I wish I felt more at home anywhere. I feel I don't have to explain myself to you that thoughts of home keep taking me back to Black Lives Matter. I wish the Black Lives Matter movement felt less relevant today than when Trayvon died. I wish Trayvon was alive today to hear his name still being spoken. I wish there weren't so many more names to say. I wish these things sincerely but I also don't remember all the other names there are to say. I can't hold them all in my head. I have to look them up when I write about them. My search phrases feel shameful, imprecise, and cavalier. Alabama church bombing. Charleston church shooting. Police brutality deaths. Police brutality victims.

As I close this letter to you, I'm seeing news of thousands of people in Hong Kong defying the police to gather for the annual vigil in memory of the victims of the Tiananmen Square massacre. There, American flags are still being held high by protesters as a symbol of democracy. All the while, protests for the Black Lives Matter movement in my first adopted home are spreading here, to my second adopted home, and I feel strongly that the flag should burn, just as strongly as the inspiration I feel from it as the symbol for freedom for Hong Kong. There are many voices daring to express that this time things feel different. The momentum, the urgency, the movements on the streets and on the whole feel different. Many leading voices belong to students in higher education and I am proud and grateful to be a part of this international community. We hold our hope in a complex space, trying our best to take responsibility for making sure that what feels different this time stays different.

A collection of Toni Morrison's nonfiction writings is entitled *Mouth Full of Blood* (2019). In her eulogy for James Baldwin, Morrison writes:

> I never heard a single command from you, yet the demands you made on me, the challenges you issued to me were nevertheless unmistakable if unenforced: that I work and think at the top of my form; that I stand on moral ground but know that ground must be shored up by mercy; "that the world is before [me] and [I] need not take it or leave it as it was when [I] came in."

I don't have to tell you that Breonna Taylor, Ahmaud Arbery, and George Floyd won't be the last to be murdered for being Black. And what about Elijah McClain? Amid all this, how do we account for the way some deaths hit us harder? When I saw Elijah's photographs, his shy and bright smile, the way he so lovingly held his violin, I felt the most irrational grief as if one of my own students had been murdered. What does it mean for me to feel this way? Does it matter? If so, why?

I don't have to tell you that I'm not sure anymore that there will come a time we can look back and say: At least there was justice, if not peace. I thought of you because I hope we can stay loud about it until that time comes, and then I hope we can take in all the air our lungs can hold, and get louder after that.

김수진 올림
June 4, 2020

정오빠 에게,

Once, I wrote a short story about you and my teeth. I built the story around a scene of you comforting me when I lost my first tooth. I imagined you as a sensitive child who loved art. You were a sensitive child, clearly, but I don't remember if you particularly loved art.

My mom says you loved exercise. You had dreams of becoming a bodybuilder. She still talks about how you turned up at our apartment in Seoul one day to surprise her with a pair of small hand-weights because you wanted her to stay strong. She'd just had me. It was all my crying that cut your visit short.

Sometimes I don't know what to do with this fury—at our mothers and our fathers and our aunts and our uncles—and grandmother, who was alive for your death, I think. Was she? 정오빠, 오빠, I can't remember now. But then I realize I do nothing with my anger all the time, though sometimes I write and I cry as I write.

I realize I don't know and/or forget important things all the time. Sometimes I want to ask my mother: When exactly did grandmother die? What became of her ashes? But I hate making my mother cry.

정오빠, I don't even know if you were buried or burned anew. I imagine there was a fight. Our Buddhist grandmother. Your then-Catholic father—who last I heard was Buddhist again and raising rodents and studying poetry. I still have the prayer beads your father gave me during his last bout of Buddhism, the ones he said a monk carved by hand during a vow of silence, the prayer beads your father pressed into my palm the last time I saw you in your narrow room with a single window.

He's fine, he's fine, our mothers said as they ushered me away from you. He's OK.

My last words to you were, "오빠, 괜찮아?"

I still fall into spirals of imagining I save you, somehow, on that day. I cry and refuse to leave until the adults let me take you to see a doctor. I bring you to America. I get you to speak. You thank me and we are OK. You help my dad at the ice-cream store, the strong son he and my mother never had. You do all the heavy lifting for him with ease. You take to the work, and you come to really love it, ice cream and the people, our life in America. I breathe a little easier knowing you are there to help me take care of my parents. One day, my dad will pass the business on to you.

My unselfish wish for you is this: I hope you meet our grandfather. May he shake your hand before he holds you close. I know he must be so proud of you, his oldest grandchild who is a grandson, a daughter's son to undo his disappointment in her. May you spend as long as you need in his embrace, having nothing asked of you and beloved. May our grandfather invite you to be birds together. Herons, maybe. Or may you be somewhere temperate, enjoying a long and beautiful meal with grandfather and grandmother, your mother and big aunt, and as you wait for the rest of us, the women will laugh about the days they saw you babbling in diapers while grandfather will say he was sorry to miss it, but that he will give you all the love and care you were due then, now, and forever. May he do so for you. May you find such serenity that it will be impossible to say which is more freeing for your soul, sitting down to that nourishing meal full of laughter and adoration or taking flight with the slow beat of your broad wings, your bones hollowed and unburdened. Maybe you can do both at once where you are.

One day, I hope I dream of you, and maybe some things will be clearer then.

수진이

한녀 [Woamn, White]

DRAMATIS PERSONAE

THE STUDENT, *a Ph.D. candidate studying abroad*
THE INSTRUCTOR, *a junior academic on probation*
YOU, *a character in a Korean drama*
NEON VERNACULAR, *a seminal text by Yusef Komunyakaa published in 1993*
TWENTY CONTESTENTS OF THE 2013 MISS KOREA PAGEANT, *a spectral chorus*

I. 곡성 [AN OPEN FIRE]

Manchester, UK. A studio flat in Chinatown. THE STUDENT *is in bed holding a well-worn copy of* NEON VERNACULAR *to her chest. There's a pen between her teeth. Beside her is a yellow legal pad, flipped to a page filled messily with half thoughts, mostly fragments from Komunyakaa's work.*

The student thinks often of a dead white woman she knows and how her killers were two Black men. When the student thinks about Eve's death, she thinks more about the two Black men and how they got caught because they told people about Eve, asking them to pray with her before they killed her. The student didn't know Eve when she was alive, but after her murder, the student was out late one night, walking across an unusually quiet and empty campus, when she found a rain-soaked photograph of her on the ground outside of the student union building. The student imagines someone who had feelings for Eve meant to say a private goodbye to her. Only someone who had a lot of feelings for her wouldn't have thought through leaving her out in the rain like that, to get stepped on, her face gone damp and distorted like that.

The student, she would have burned her photograph in an open fire, smoke rising to the sky, along with something they both loved, for her to take with her to that other place.

II. 여교수 [LANGUAGE OF FLOWERS]

London, UK. An academic office in Bloomsbury. THE INSTRUCTOR *is holding out a box of tissues with both hands to a figure seated on her sofa. She is trying to maintain a neutral expression.*

In the classroom, the instructor finds herself saying things like, "This scene makes me wonder if this was the first big death she experienced in her life."

When the instructor thinks of death, she often thinks of white women. Yusef Komunyakaa writes, "Stopped in this garden, / Drawn to some Lotus-eater." The subtitles say:

[A black man is singing, "I'm here, as if I never left," a work song.]

The instructor thinks of the white woman she upset in her second year of teaching in a precarious position, trying to teach someone else's syllabus as if it were her own. She was leading a seminar on *Pride and Prejudice*. She asked the students to consider that the last few lines of the novel saw Lizzy compared to "pollution." "I disagree," the white woman said. "This is a love story. This is the most famous love story in the world." The white woman was respectful, polite, firm in her conviction, yet tremulous. The instructor wanted to ask her what exactly the white woman was disagreeing with, but she feared the white woman would cry.

It was the same year the instructor felt she had to tell her students: It's OK to say Black. She was leading a seminar on *Heart of Darkness*. The instructor said, "It's OK to say someone is Black." That was when the instructor learned to hold the silence.

The instructor learned to be more careful, evermore, fixing her gaze to a white woman's watery blue eyes. The instructor writes her own syllabuses now, sometimes, but she holds on to a ghost: pale polite hair, pale polite face. The visitations grow more unsettling each time. She swears, all those years ago, she was wearing white.

III. 여학생 [SHE PUTS SOMETHING ON]

Manchester, UK. A studio flat in Chinatown. THE STUDENT *is still in bed but with an open laptop now, staring at Yusef Komunyakaa's Wikipedia page and wondering what the actual hell she is doing with her life.*

There is a book the student loves deeply. She has read it many times. She longs to inhabit the text as her own. But it's complicated.

When she tries to write about it, she fears she is not herself—or something worse. When she tries to write about this fear, the student feels further distracted. But the fear, she thinks, must be a part of it, too, her deep love for a book that is and is not hers. Must she claim it out loud? If so, how? What are the words she must say? What are the words?

The student doesn't want to read or write anymore. She opens a new tab. She puts something on. A woman in white stands at the river's edge. She clicks the subtitles off, then on again.

IV. 우리 [VOICES OF LITTLE GIRLS]

Seoul, Korea. A grand hotel lobby and, later, a 포장마차. YOU move about fretfully, frenetically.

You are a tertiary female character in a Korean drama. You are small and all your clothes are oversized. You wear a lot of pastel. Your hair is always in slight disarray and your wide-lens glasses distract from your face. You are in your thirties but you have the voice of a child, rather, how we are taught to imagine the voices of little girls.

You are wed, briefly, to a humorless man. In the tail end of the reception, you discover your ceremonial husband kissing another woman with a kind of passion always denied to you. You flee from the sight and he chases you through the hotel lobby to inform you, loudly, in that grand, resonant space, that he never loved you. He says he was only following the advice of his mother to marry a simple, somewhat stupid girl who would serve him well.

Time passes with the central arc of the drama. Now you are confessing to the secondary male lead that you wanted to kill yourself that night of your wedding. You fixed your gaze to the 한. You took your shoes off.

Your voice is raised and tremulous. You have no idea how girlish you sound. You have no idea that when you speak, the music that plays is a jaunty, tinkling piano tune, a parody of ragtime without any sadness in the soul, or perhaps without any soul at all.

This is the nature of your sincerity. You do not know that this scene is not about you or your desire to die. This scene is about the secondary male lead realizing he is attracted to you.

V. 한놈 [HOW THE WORLD WORKS]

A continuum. TWENTY CONTESTANTS OF THE 2013 MISS KOREA PAGEANT *stand in a circle and scream into the center endlessly.*

In 2014, a white male professor from Princeton declared, "After the near-collapse of the world's financial system has shown that we economists really do not know how the world works, I am much too embarrassed to teach economics anymore, which I have done for many years. I will teach *Modern Korean Drama* instead."

In a mock proposal for such a class, the white male professor writes, "Although I have never been to Korea, I have watched Korean drama on a daily basis for over six years now. Therefore I can justly consider myself an expert in that subject."

배수아 writes in <뱀과 물> (2017):

전혀 피곤하지 않았지만 이상하게도 나는 어느새 잠이 들었다. 그리고 내가 잠이 들자마자, 여자 심리학자가 와서 나를 흔들어 깨웠으므로 나는 아무런 꿈도 꾸지 못한 채 다시 눈을 떴다. 창밖은 여전히 어두웠다. 여자 심리학자는 방을 나가기 전과 똑같이 두건이 달린 검은 외투 차림이었다.

"지금 떠나야 해." 여자 심리학자가 서둘렀다. "지금 널
태우고 갈 트럭이 밖에서 기다리고 있어."
"이제 꿈이 시작되는 건가요?"
"바보 같은 소리 하지 마라."

The white male professor's proposal went viral in the wake of a series of
official headshots for the twenty contestants of the 2013 Miss Daegu
pageant making similar rounds, inviting derision of the women for
looking all the same due to the grotesquery of plastic surgery.

In addition to widely mislabeling the twenty women as finalists of
the 2013 Miss Korea pageant, articles purporting to reveal a more
true-to-life group photo of the women from Daegu used an image
of twenty contestants from the 2013 Miss Seoul pageant instead.
These errors remain largely uncorrected or glossed over, even in
follow-ups with more images of the twenty women from Daegu who
were further tasked with posing in what is described as their more
natural states, more real, more human, these women, twenty in all,
still holding their smiles, still holding their assigned numbers to be
identified.

The white male professor writes, "The overall impression conveyed
by a good modern Korean drama is of a land of truly handsome men
and exceptionally beautiful, fashionable women. Korean women
remain quite beautiful even after plastic surgeons have retrofitted
their original, even more beautiful original Asian faces with pointed
and straight Western noses and Western eyelids."

The subtitles say:

[Is the dream starting now?
Don't be stupid.]

VI. 우리 [ONE OF YOU MUST CHANGE]

Seoul, Korea. By the 한강 *and, later, a* 포장마차. YOU *move about fretfully, frenetically.*

In this scene, you are arguing with a woman who looks like you. She is possibly one of a number of your sisters, or she is your mother, or she is your aunt, or she is one of your sisters' mothers-in-law, or she is your frenemy who deleted your presentation slides, stealing your one chance at a promotion, or she is your husband's mistress. You are both standing ankle-deep by the bank of the 한. Your hair is long and dark. Your dress is long and white. One of you must change.

Your fight bears no consequence on the central arc. The piano music when you speak, even when you are shouting, is louder than you.

You remind the woman who looks like you that you are a kind of doctor.

The woman who looks like you shouts for you to take the bones out of your words.

The subtitles say:

[Don't be sarcastic!]

You fix your gaze to the once-soft spot between the eyes of the woman who looks like you and you think of that time you started saying something angry to a white man for comparing you to his Asian girlfriend, and a white woman interrupted you to tell you, "Be nice!"

You change. You blow out your hair. You put on new shoes and seek solace in drinks with the secondary male lead. He has been neither married nor divorced and is a dental surgeon of some international renown. You drink and stare longingly into each other's original, even more beautiful original Asian faces with your Asian eyes and Asian noses. The more you drink, the more bones grow inside your words.

VII. ON KOREAN LOVE [THE GRAVE DANGER]

Manchester, UK. A studio flat in Chinatown. THE STUDENT *sits up in bed, startled, wondering where the screaming is coming from.*

On Korean love, the white male professor writes of controlling and prejudiced Korean mothers determined to separate the star-crossed. He notes, "[As] a last desperate resort, there is always the announcement that one or the other of the two young lovers will be sent to study in America, which seems to be the dumping ground for the young Koreans who have fallen in love without their mother's permission. Rarely do the mothers realize the grave danger to which they thus expose their offspring—the possibility that in America the offspring might fall in love with and marry someone other than a Korean."

He pairs this with an image of an Asian man with a white woman, followed by an image of a white man with an Asian woman. These are not stills from a drama. This is the white male professor's balanced, real-world texture. The student accepts it is her inability to estimate the ages of white people that makes the white man look so much older than the Asian woman next to him. The student quells the instant hate for his lobster-red face and low open collar, that stupid heavy chain around his thick neck. The student accepts that the Asian man and Asian woman are Korean, according to their original, even more beautiful original Asian faces with their Asian eyes and Asian noses. The student accepts that the white man and white woman are American.

VIII. 여학생 [SOMETHING MORE SENSELESS]

Manchester, UK. A studio flat in Chinatown. THE STUDENT *holds* NEON VERNACULAR *close as she pulls the covers over her head and closes her eyes, wondering if anyone else can hear it, all that screaming.*

The opening line of Wilkie Collins's *The Woman in White* states, "This is the story of what a Woman's patience can endure, and what a Man's resolution can achieve." The student notes that the woman in white is a personification of the fascination with how bodies relate to society. The student notes that the woman in white flits in and out of the narrative, embodies a death-in-life ambiguity, and renders the world oddly spectral.

Edgar Allan Poe writes, "The death [. . .] of a beautiful woman is unquestionably the most poetical topic in the world, and equally is it beyond doubt that the lips best suited for such topic are those of a bereaved lover," and the student notes this, too, and wonders if the fucking small-mouthed, lily-handed creep must reach in and grab white women in a particular way that the student cannot fully understand.

The student is compelled to study the shadow of the woman in white and finds it to be an impression. Yusef Komunyakaa writes, "As if gods wrestled here."

In "Work," the man of resolution is a hired Black man working the garden of his mistress, who wears her whiteness like a trap. Instead of unexpected visitations, the white woman lies deathly still in the full light of day, in the garden of an antebellum house that:

> Looms behind oak & pine
> Like a secret, as quail
> Flash through branches.

This is the Deep South evoking the hunt of Old World Europe. This is Oxford, Mississippi. Through Komunyakaa's working, the landscape so steeped in tragic traditions is also a jungle of the Eastern world at once:

> Leaning into the lawnmower's
> Roar through pine needles
> & crabgrass. Tiger-colored
> Bumblebees nudge pale blossoms
> Till they sway like silent bells
> Calling. But I won't look.

Exoticism is the word the student spits and chases with salt, suggestive of an otherworldly warring, but at heart the student resists overt connections to the Vietnam War, as tempting as it is with Komunyakaa's service as a war correspondent and later editor for a military newspaper that earned him a Bronze Star. The student knows that the image of tigers in jungles is more storybook than history. More so than the nightmare of the Vietnam War seeping into the suburban scene, hellish suburbia invades the Black imagination, mutating familiar terrains into the lush rot of a Southern Gothic, distorting the histories of wars, wars, wars into something more senseless than before. The student knows. Or, at least, she suspects.

IX. 한놈 [A FASCINATING HISTORY]

A continuum. TWENTY CONTESTANTS OF THE 2013 MISS KOREA PAGEANT *are still here, still standing in a circle and still screaming into the center—endlessly. This is what "endlessly" means.*

The white male professor clarifies that most of the Korean dramas he watches are historical. "I find it to be a fascinating history that should be known more widely in the world," he says. He praises the ability of Korean actors, particularly the ability to cry on command.

He notes, however:

> Often the endings of a drama series are let-downs. They seem hastily contrived and are often a bit corny (as we would put it). I think even I, an economist, could do better.

> Furthermore, forgiveness of even the most egregious behavior seems to be a theme in Korean dramas. Sometimes one wishes that the really bad characters would be punished more. Is forgiveness of this sort really a reality in Korea?

X. 여학생 [WHITENESS FORETOLD]

Manchester, UK. A studio flat in Chinatown. THE STUDENT *runs the pad of her thumb along the edges of* NEON VERNACULAR, *knowing by feel which folded indent marks what poem.*

The impression is a shallow bed-grave with space only for immediacy and baseness. The woman in white is reduced to this glaring image:

I won't look at her. Nude
On a hammock among elephant ears
& ferns, a pitcher of lemonade
Sweating like our skin.

"Nude" is the only word directly describing the white woman in the entire poem. This degradation unites her with the Black man through "our skin." Though the Black man resolves again and again throughout the poem, "I won't look at her," the blinding color of her is all he sees and understands of the white woman directly.

The rest of her is imagined through details of the domestic world around her. Even the details of her body beyond the whiteness of her skin must be further imagined through the landscape. Her eyes blue as "Afternoon burns on the pool / Till everything's blue." Her hair golden as the summer heat, as fine as the pale daffodils. Even the idea of summer must be inferred from the lushness of the jungle garden around her, from the "Scent of honeysuckle." She sits like a glowing fruit amid the elephant ears and ferns. The curves of her figure are detailed only through the fat pitcher of lemonade, the taste of her imagined sweetly, quenching a thirst, yet shudderingly sour, shockingly chilling amid the Mississippi summer heat, as is the foreboding luminosity of her whiteness foretold by the pale blossoms that toll of death.

Kate Daniels writes, "When Komunyakaa's gaze settles on white women, I find myself represented in ways I can't tolerate."

Natasha D. Trethewey writes, "Perhaps Daniels was too busy seeing herself [. . .] as opposed to losing herself in the world of the poem to give it the close reading it deserves."

Speaking only through the color of her skin, the white woman is a stagnant and largely imagined thing, a still life framed by the domestic world around her. As poetic as Poe could ever hope for, she is so much an object of art that she may as well be dead. She is fixed here, unlike her nameless husband who is offstage, unlike the idyllic gesture of "daughter & son" neatly marking her nameless children as archetypal as the flashy cars they drive off in, unlike even Roberta the cook who is off for the day:

> Her husband's outside Oxford,
> Mississippi, bidding on miles
> Of timber. I wonder if he's buying
> Faulkner's ghost, if he might run
> Into Colonel Sartoris
> Along some dusty road.
> Their teenage daughter & son sped off
> An hour ago in a red Corvette
> For the tennis courts,
> & the cook, Roberta,
> Only works a half day
> Saturdays.

Roberta's absence serves as a marker of time, albeit in strange increments of "a half day," as the only reliable evidence that time is, indeed, passing. Roberta is also the only person of the household, but not family, named in the poem. Her role and her naming have no more significance than that of the flora and fauna around the white woman, itemized along with the trappings of wealth, alongside the plants, flowers, and creatures surrounding the mistress of the house as props, or, more suggestively, as ingredients laid out for a working.

The student reads the poem as a spell.

> Black magic lurks in the shadow of the antebellum house.
> Black magic lurks in the shadow of the antebellum house.
> Black magic lurks in the shadow of the antebellum house.

The cursed aristocratic family on their cursed land are decaying time immemorial, "Along some dusty road," it doesn't really matter where exactly, as long as it's a place like Oxford, Mississippi.

Here, Faulkner's ghost holds no more power than the fictional Confederate Colonel Sartoris who, in turn, holds no more power than Roberta the cook. Their ineffectual trinity offers no resurrection for the woman wearing her whiteness. The only named entity with semblance of agency, of all the entities haunting southern soil that could have been invoked, is Johnny Mathis on the radio. The unexpected apparition of the jazzy pop singer serves as a bizarrely fitting oracle, his whisper signaling the turning point of the poem:

> Afternoon burns on the pool
> Till everything's blue,
> Till I hear Johnny Mathis
> Beside her like a whisper.
> I work all the quick hooks
> Of light, the same unbroken
> Rhythm my father taught me
> Years ago: *Always give*
> *A man a good day's labor.*
> I won't look. The engine
> Pulls me like a dare.

The student finds comfort in the black humor of the bard of jazzy pop cast as some sort of spirit medium invoking the parable-like words of the speaker's father, crooning impending doom. The student is moved by irreverence. The strangeness of this casting is in the vein of the beastliness of bumblebees in the jungle garden, the way a sweaty pitcher of lemonade speaks of sex, gender, and race heavy-handedly, as the student does, as the student longs to, but also of how "our skin" must be cool to the touch, corpselike, in spite of and especially because of the contrast to the southern summer heat, the cool glass reflecting the ambiguity of death-in-life.

The student listens to the jazzy pop of a closeted, then, outed gay Black man and reflects on language as our public and private selves.

XI. 여학생 [DIALS A NUMBER]

Manchester, UK. A studio flat in Chinatown. THE STUDENT *opens her eyes. She throws off the covers but keeps* NEON VERNACULAR *close. She takes a deep breath, all the air her lungs can hold. She screams back.*

The student is in the final year of writing up her doctoral thesis when her family nearly goes bankrupt. The student desperately needs to go home to be with her parents who can't speak English very well. She is sitting in her supervisor's office trying to find the right words for the situation. She wants to protect her parents. She wants to protect herself. The student has learned to be careful in how she presents herself. She is careful, asking about the possibility of time off and who she ought to consult regarding possible complications with her visa.

"Why aren't you crying?" her supervisor asks her. "You should be crying, talking about these things."

The student does not know what to say.

"You are depressed," her supervisor says.

The student tries to explain everything again, that what she needs from the meeting today is— As the student is speaking, the supervisor picks up the phone on his desk and dials a number. The student does not understand, but the supervisor is already speaking to whoever is on the end of the line, saying, "Yes, I need to report a student who is depressed."

The student longs for a body of water. She longs for a body.

XII. 한놈 [FERTILE AND BREATHTAKINGLY BEAUTIFUL]

A continuum. TWENTY CONTESTANTS OF THE 2013 MISS KOREA PAGEANT *are screaming even louder now.*

Of a family losing all of its savings and its house, the white male professor writes, "It will cause much 'stress.' Finance gone awry always is a major stress-begetter in Korean drama, which is why it always is part of a good drama." There is no explanation for why stress is in quotes.

Instead, the white male professor explains that Koreans react to "stress" in mysterious ways such as seeking medical attention, drinking, and going outdoors with a particular penchant for standing next to and staring at "some river bank or ocean beach."

The white male professor notes, "Koreans inhabit a land that is both fertile and breathtakingly beautiful. Yet, endowed with all of these blessings, the Koreans in these dramas seem to spend all day and night making one another miserable and sending to God several million sighed 'Aigoohs' every day. What a pity!"

In an interview for the *Korea Times*, the white male professor says his proposal for Modern Korean Drama was "impromptu," meant to "entertain" a conference of "health insurance experts" from Korea and Taiwan.

"Actually I do not teach such a course, but economics instead," he says.

XIII. 우리 [WHAT YOUR FATHER TAUGHT YOU]

Seoul, Korea. A modest home in the suburbs, but later YOU *will end up at a* 포장마차 *again.* YOU *are screaming now, too.* YOU *have always been screaming.*

A pair of gangsters in black suits turn up at your house, armed with steel pipes. They work for the merciless loan shark your father is indebted to. You are the one stupid enough to answer the door. One of the gangsters takes off his jacket and rolls up his sleeves to better swing his pipe around and to show off his tattoos, tigers and dragons that look more like blue-veined snakes. He doesn't hit anything yet, but it's not hard to imagine the sound of a bone cracking; you can call it forth just as you would the imagined voice of a little girl. The gangsters want to know if your father is home, but you are home alone, it's just you and a number of women who look like you. The women are hiding behind the curtains, in the wardrobes, beneath the bed. Some are under the floorboards, mouths wide, hoping for something nourishing to seep through the gaps. There are women in the drains, too, but you cannot bear to think of them right now.

You ask the gangsters if they have mothers, sisters, wives, girlfriends, any women in their lives who matter to them, and/or daughters. This is what your father taught you to ask them. You beg them to not kill you or the nineteen other women who look like you until you can all be mothers to shining sons. This is how your father taught you to beg. You sob as you vow that your sons will be better than your father who is not home. Your father who is not home has never been home, not once, but your sons, they will be, each son a two, no, three-story home, each son a home, each son a mansion. This is what your father taught you to vow. Your bony words are choking you. You sob until the gangsters leave. Instead of piano music is the sound of the men sucking their teeth.

XIV. 여학생 [BRIGHT JEWEL TONES]

Manchester, UK. A studio flat in Chinatown. THE STUDENT *understands she has always been screaming, too. She feels herself untethering from the fabric of space-time. She feels as if* NEON VERNACULAR *may be screaming with her, but what* NEON VERNACULAR *is trying to tell her is that we are traveling from time to eternity.*

If narcissus tolls of death, cinnabar insinuates how violent the deaths will be. The clarion call of an unnamed Johnny Mathis song with its "quick hooks" and "unbroken rhythm" gives way to the "Scent of honeysuckle" that bleeds into:

Sings black sap through mystery,
Taboo, law, creed, what kills
A fire that is its own heart
Burning open the mouth.

The culmination of "Work" is not the act of transgression between the white woman and Black man but what follows—the "Gasoline & oil" that takes us to the end.

The husband offstage who is bidding "on miles / Of timber" is part of the aftermath. The husband is an audacious man who swears oaths, and wears his whiteness as a badge, as a mask. He drives nails into miles of timber, he stakes it all into the red earth, and he sets everything ablaze.

The student thinks about the many field trips she took to the Levine Museum of the New South, the many relics they have on display there, the pristine masks, the shining robes, not all white at all, but bright jewel tones for the highest ordained. Where did they come from, these robes, these masks? How and why were they so perfectly preserved? Whose hands continue to care for them?

The Black man cannot account for the aftermath of the transgression of two mere bodies. As "Work" closes, he "can't say why," voiceless altogether.

XV. 여교수 [HANG THEIR HEADS]

London, UK. An attic flat in the suburbs. THE INSTRUCTOR *unclenches her jaw.*

The instructor is lying in her bed, clutching her phone. She is waiting for a call. It is three a.m. She thinks of the editor from that magazine who wrote back within hours to say that he had no time to read her essay, and besides, he wasn't sure if their website could support Korean characters. The instructor thinks about her first time meeting an editor from a major publishing house, who came to visit a writing class during her master's. When asked what the editor was looking for, the editor's response was that it was easier to say what she was not looking for. For example, the editor was currently editing a book by a Korean American woman, so she wasn't looking for any more Korean books for the next year or so. The instructor thinks about the roomful of eyes turning on her, all eyes except the editor's. The instructor thinks about how careful the editor was to not see her for the whole of the hour.

Had she a book, she is unsure what is the name, what is the name she would put to it. What she remembers best about Korea is the recurring dream of a pale snake outside her bedroom window, calling her name. The name she thought could be cut away from her like tonsils, a kidney, a spleen. She knew not to answer it then, but if she heard that low, soft beckoning now, she fears she would surrender. She fears she would say, Yes, I will reside in the thin fleshy walls of you, slick with your venom; it is what I have always wanted, nothing more than to succumb to slow decay amid all the soft, blooded things, and, too, all the fine, sharp parts inside a snake.

The instructor whispers into the glassy dark surface of her phone: Narcissus is the namesake of Echo's doomed love for a beautiful and stupid boy. It is the flower that lured young and sweet Proserpine to the dark embrace of Pluto. The *Narcissus tazetta* is sometimes cited as the Rose of Sharon, the flower symbolic of Christ from the Song of Solomon. Victorian folklore dictates that daffodils do not belong in the domestic space for the way they hang their heads, bringing tears and unhappiness, and are as pale as death. The narcissus is relegated as a grave flower befitting only the decoration of a final resting place. The Lotos-eater speaks in a language of flowers. Lush rot, lush rot, it was not you who put these words together. You need to cite your sources. You need to read Tennyson.

XVI. 여학생 [RAISES HER HAND]

Manchester, UK. Or maybe London. A studio flat in Chinatown. Or maybe a classroom in Bloomsbury. THE STUDENT's *phone alarm goes off. She can barely hear it over the screaming, but it's time to call her mom.*

The student raises her hand and says, "It's Roberta I'm worried about."

The year of Eve's death is also when the student tries to make more friends by attending an interest meeting for a society for English majors. The faculty advisor is a professor the student has never met before, but she knows how to read a room, sometimes. The student wonders if he's a famous author. The author of—*Big Tree?*—teaches at her university, but she's pretty sure this isn't him.

The faculty advisor says, Let's talk about what we can do as a group, a collective, if you will. How can we make an impact? How can we bring about change?

The student dares to fill the silence. She is genuinely excited. It would be so helpful, she says, if we could organize a way to share and exchange textbooks among ourselves. The student thinks the part she doesn't need to say out loud is that this term alone, she has spent over $800 on textbooks.

The student has hardly finished speaking when the faculty advisor says no. NO, he says it again. Louder this time.

He says, I'm speaking to higher concepts than that. I'm interested in the performance of our—actually, the student, no, NO—the instructor now—the instructor doesn't remember exactly what the man says anymore.

In this scene, trying to write this goddamn essay, when the instructor tries really hard to really really remember what it was that this goddamn faculty advisor said after his no—NO—what surfaces is the memory of seeing the first human shit other than her own. The instructor must have been a toddler. She was still in Korea. Her parents took her camping in the mountains (but not the mountains in which her mother grew up) and her dad was guiding her by the hand to take her somewhere she could shit. She remembers it so vividly, squatting by her dad's feet and studying that small, quiet clearing, fixing her gaze to the middle distance, where thick coils of sickly green-brown shit were piled up in such a mound, like a baby's grave, crawling with luminescent green bottle flies. Thankfully, the instructor recalls no scent, just the childish sense of wonder at how anyone could possibly produce so much shit.

The instructor remembers that the faculty advisor spent the rest of the meeting talking about videos he was making of screen recordings on his MacBook Pro, describing his tendency to have too many tabs open at once while working on his research, while writing his book. The instructor remembers his mouth sounds about performance? Technology? Attention? Something about human attention. She remembers best his certainty of his authority on human attention, his sureness that his experience of the digital age was so profound that it had to be universal, coming from him, it had to be.

XVII. WOAMN [WHERE THE SICK LIE]

London, UK. A classroom in Bloomsbury. THE INSTRUCTOR's *phone alarm goes off.* THE STUDENT *is lost in a continuum.* THE INSTRUCTOR *apologizes and turns off her phone.*

In 1997, bell hooks wrote in "Representing Whiteness in the Black Imagination," "If the mask of whiteness, the pretense, represents it as always benign, benevolent, then what this representation obscures is the representation of danger, the sense of threat."

In 1977, Yusef Komunyakaa published the first issue of a nonprofit literary magazine founded in Fort Collins, Colorado. The first issue of *Gumbo* contains a poem by Gloria Watkins called "Where the Sick Lie":

> death is
> always asleep
> in the middle
> room
> feather mattress
> feather pillows
> bed that rocks
> like a boat
> I fear the
> water
> black folk

can't swim
in the room
she lie
blood in the
wash pan
empty this
dream
a bed of water
fat old woamn
chewing tobacco
Death in
the spitoon

The student raises her hand and says, "Was 'woamn' intentional?"

The instructor says, "We are animal. This is a poem."

XVIII. 우리 [GREEN AND GOLD AND MUD]

Seoul, Korea. YOU *just want to go home, but* YOU *don't want to be the one to say so. Home is—where, exactly?* 우리 한강갈까 포장마차갈까? 아이씨 모르겠다, 곡이나 부르자. 아, 아, 아 맞다, 엄마한테 전화해야지.

In this scene, you are at a conference attended entirely by women who look like you, women who are you, but, of course, your frenemy has deleted your presentation slides. You must speak "impromptu" and "entertain." You were never going to get a promotion, anyway.

This is what you say:

Our home has many occupants: mother, father, black cat, black snake, and me. Black dog is buried in the garden, beneath stones we brought down from the mountains (but not the mountains mother grew up in).

Mother's work is in the fields, ankle-deep in wet dark earth shot through with green. Father's role is to reap what she sows.

Father says, "Do your job well."

Mother says, "Terrible things will happen if you don't."

It is up to me to keep black cat and black snake from eating one another. Black cat is soft and sleeps small ball in my lap. I am cruel to black snake. Ugly black snake, long as I am tall.

One day, black snake runs away.

I run into the fields and I call out for black snake. "뱀!" I call, "뱀!" I slap my thigh with the flat of my hand as I would when I call for black cat, but this method only ever worked with black dog. Still, I stand in the center of the green and gold and mud and call out for black snake. "뱀! 뱀! 뱀!" I must bring her home.

But when I call, I see that the ground is made up entirely of snakes. They are packed tight and writhing all together toward the horizon. One is as wide as my body is long, patterned in copper and verdigris. I follow the slow pulse of her body as far as my eye can see, but cannot see her tail beyond the horizon.

This is what the subtitles say:

[A woman in white rises from the water, wailing.
Snakes are pouring out of her mouth.
This is a traditional Korean story, and she is looking for an ending.]

XIX. 한녀 [WE JUST CALL THEM DRAMAS]

A continuum. TWENTY CONTESTANTS OF THE 2013 MISS KOREA
PAGEANT *standing in a circle are joined by* YOU *who can't find the
way home and* THE STUDENT *holding* NEON VERNACULAR *close,
endlessly. All of the women are still screaming.* THE INSTRUCTOR
*materializes in the center of the circle and begins to weave through the
crowd without really noticing where she is or where she is going. She
has her phone pressed hard to one ear. In the other is her finger, poised
like the barrel of a gun.*

엄마! 엄마 나야. 엄마 잘 들려? 아, 아니야, 안 바빠.

We are Korean omen. We are either too fat or too thin. Our Korean
mother will tell us one or the other. She will never tell us that our
body is beautiful, that we are beautiful. She will never tell us that
we are perfect the way we are. She will, however, tell us that our
body is important. She will tell us to take great care with our body.
몸조심, 또 몸조심. She will tell us that health is best, health is
first, health is everything, but the soundest translation will be
our mother telling us to just stay alive. This is when we know that
things are very, very bad.

This is the ending we have been searching for. We collate six
photographs and add our own to round out the circle of seven: our
sister, our mother, our aunt, our sisters' mother-in-law, our frenemy
who deleted our presentation slides, and our husband's mistress,

and we who have been searching. We will disseminate this image. We, too, will circulate. If we're lucky, we'll go viral. We will no longer be told that what is unspeakable is unintelligible. And we will have words to say, then, about our diminutive and interchangeable selves.

밥? 밥 먹었지. 먹었다니까.

The subtitles will say:

[Please could you kindly rethink your takes on Asian women?]

엄마? 여보세요? 엄마?

엄마?

This is the ending we have been waiting for, six dead women who look like us. Be grateful it is not more. Our mom becomes sick. We tell ourselves that her fever is from the vaccine, but we know she is seeing the self she could have been in the photo of the mother with her smiling sons. We know she is seeing us in a daughter left behind. We tell her it's not her. We tell her it's not us. We tell ourselves these things, too. They are not us, these women. But everything is difficult to remember. We want to keep her on the line, our mother. We ask her what she's watching. We ask her about any good dramas. Between us, we just call them dramas. We learned to love them from her. But lately, our mother says: nothing, I don't watch dramas anymore. They make me too angry. They make me too sad. We are silent for a long while, us and our mother. We want to keep her on the line. We ask her about the mountains she grew up in, but it is we who start telling the story of a man who gets lost in the mountains. Deep into the night, he roams desperately through the dense woods until he comes across a woman in white who offers him a cool drink of water from a stone cup. He does not hesitate to accept. She is beautiful and he is thirsty. When he drinks, it is the most refreshing, satisfying thing he has ever tasted. He drinks and drinks from her stone cup. He drinks until the sun rises. In the full daylight, his vision shifts, and the woman in white is gone, but he is still holding her stone cup. The cup is full of blood. He can taste the thickness now. He can taste the salt and metallic tang. It's coating his teeth, his tongue, his throat. His belly is full of blood. He can feel it sloshing. More still is dripping into the dark stone cup. The man looks up into the branches and above hangs a freshly skinned snake, its tail in a knot. Milk-eyed and openmouthed, it drips, and drips.

Our mother is still there, on the end of the line. Time passes with the central arc of the drama. We are still here, writing our own syllabuses sometimes. 아이구, 이 한심한년아 ―

마음 [Home Without Mom]

MOTHER

Loudly, brokenly.

If I die first, how will you take care of your father? Look how he grows thin. He fusses about everything I cook. Now he says rice is too heavy for breakfast. He eats like a child. Who eats an entire box of HoHos and calls it a light breakfast? What is wrong with him? Do you think he does this to me on purpose? Is he trying to make me miserable? Do you think he's trying to kill me with my own fury? I am going to die first. Some vein, some vessel is sure to burst inside me. Maybe an artery. Do you know what an artery is? You never would've cut it as a real doctor. You see blood and you pass out. You'd just let me die. And then what will you do? Look, I told him he could at least do the dishes, and just look. No gloves. The wrong sponge. The one I told him not to use a thousand times. How will you care for him with your lack of patience, your penchant for cruelty? You will be miserable like me. You remember I told you so. Look at the way he's throwing around that rice bowl. Does he know how expensive it is? He knows. He knows. I've told him a thousand times. He doesn't care. Your father doesn't care. His head is some kind of rock formation. Igneous. Ignoble. Ignorant idiot. Do you know how many times I had to tell him to do the dishes? Look how rough his hands have grown. How rough his hands have grown, your father's hands. Have you seen your father's hands? Look. They could be hooves, his hands. They could be coarse stone, like his stupid head. All these years of dunking his bare hands in abrasive things: dish soap, bleach, ammonia, or worse. You were too young to remember his first job here at a chicken processing plant. You were too young to hear him cry out in his sleep. You never saw him tremble in the dark. He never speaks of it, how, each night, he picked out the dried blood from beneath his fingernails before seeing you, even though you were already asleep by the time he got home. He never speaks of it. Especially not to me. I've never understood your father. He never really says what's inside his stupid stone head. I'm always telling him he'll be sorry when I'm dead. You'll be sorry, too. You'll both be so sorry. But sometimes I think of the exact sound your father used to make in the dark, that long broken cry—and I'm sorry, I'm sorry, too.

Dear Manchester Chinatown, [고은정]

This is a story I have rewritten several times and told out loud many more times than that. It is also the story that prefaced my doctoral thesis against the advice of my supervisor at the time:

In the spring of 2005, my friend Molly and I decided to skip our junior prom to go ghost hunting instead. We'd both received digital cameras for Christmas and I was so lonely and insecure that I clung to her, wanting to believe that we had a bond that felt like we'd been witches together in a past life.

On a website called Shadowlands listing the most haunted places in the state, amid flashing neon text against a black and red background riddled with Halloween clip art, we found an entry on the Piney Grove AME Zion Church.

The first story we read about Piney Grove said that the church had been abandoned by its Black congregation in protest of a greedy white landlord. Another story said Piney Grove's pastor had gone mad and slit a choir girl's throat at the altar.

All we had were the stories, the name of the church, and its once-town. We knew the town by name, but it wasn't a real place to us, only the remnants of one of many such towns swallowed up by our sprawling city named after an English queen.

It didn't take long for us to get lost, but getting lost felt like a part of our plan. About two hours' drive out from the familiar limits of our city, we stopped seeing official road signs. We circled around empty fields, tall trees, and rotting power lines that filled the air with a strange hum and seemed to lead nowhere.

We stopped at the top of a hill to get our bearings, trying to figure out which way we'd come and which direction the gas station had been. Suddenly Molly gripped my shoulder. We watched through the windows as a rickety skateboard rolled uphill and stopped a few feet from the driver's-side door.

I remember a moment of silence and my ears ringing, then the two of us in wild laughter as we tried to pretend this wasn't the most thrilling and terrifying thing we could ever remember happening to us. Molly got out of the car and picked up the skateboard like it wasn't anything. She put it in the trunk, got back in the car, and just started driving in the direction the skateboard had come from. Her hands were shaking, but I thought she was so cool.

The gravel road we went down was occupied by just one house. It was an old plantation, white and decaying, surrounded by azaleas browning in the heat. We rang the doorbell without answer, so we pounded on the door with our fists and called out hellos. At last, the door creaked open to reveal a squat one-eyed man.

He wore bright red suspenders that matched the paint on his front door, and leaned heavily on a cane tipped in silver. As I asked for directions, I tried hard not to stare at the blackened skin where his right eye should have been, focusing instead on his single milky blue eye.

The one-eyed man said sure, he'd heard of Piney Grove, and drew us a map with a Mont Blanc pen from his shirt pocket and Panthers stationery from his foyer table. As he marked the location of the church with a cross, he invited us to join a backyard barbecue with his family, which was why it'd taken him a while to get to the door.

We declined because we didn't want to lose any more light. And we felt such a rush knowing that Piney Grove was really real—and that we were close. We thanked the one-eyed man and went on our way. He didn't ask us why we were headed for an abandoned church, and we didn't ask him if he had a son or a grandson who owned a skateboard.

As Molly drove on, we didn't talk about the skateboard or the one-eyed man, but his map was easy to follow. Soon we spotted a little white church with boarded-up windows.

Molly and I had grown up in the city surrounded by megachurches with congregations by the hundreds. But Piney Grove AME Zion Church looked so familiar to us, in the way nearly all of us still recognize the sun as a prickly circle, or a tree as a cloud hanging above two sticks.

The bare-boned wooden church sat in a small clearing surrounded by tall trees slowly but surely reclaiming a forest. The dirt driveway leading up to the cement-block front steps was nearly overtaken by crabgrass and clover. Molly ignored the driveway and parked the car in the small cemetery behind the church so that it couldn't be seen from the road. She was so much better at this stuff than me.

But, as much as we'd talked about breaking in somehow to take photos at the blood-stained altar, we only took a few shots of the church exterior and of interesting gravestones. I remember one image in particular of a row of children's graves right by Molly's car, all sharing a last name. We spent the remaining daylight picking dandelions and balancing them atop headstones. We shared a clove cigarette Molly had stolen from her mother as we watched the sunset. Molly said we ought to come back one day with her crowbar. Molly was a fearless driver and owned her own crowbar. Of course, I was in awe of her.

By the time we got back on the road, it was pitch-black. If you have only ever lived in cities, I can't explain that kind of dark to you, out where nothing lasts, not even God's house. We drove to the nearest gas station in silence and pulled into a lot radiant with buzzing fluorescent lights that loomed in great white discs high above our heads.

I blinked away spots as I stepped out to stretch, while Molly went in to pay. It was then that I noticed what was on the hood of Molly's car. I remember trying to call for her, to say her name out loud, but I was unable to make a sound. I stood there, in front of the car, staring at the hood until Molly came back.

She stood next to me and held my hand. Of course, I was in awe of her, how she could just take another girl's hand like that. We stared and stared until I finally managed to say, "Look." That was enough to break the spell. We got our cameras from the backseat and took photos with trembling hands.

It started to rain as we drove home. On the radio, there were flash flood warnings throughout the county. Molly and I never spoke again about that night. After high school, we grew apart, as girls who called each other best friends sometimes do.

Back when I used to tell this story on nights out over drinks, I always left out certain details, like the skateboard and the one-eyed man. They're too much. I pared the story down and got straight to

the church. I said Molly and I did break in and that we took so many
pictures, rolls and rolls of film. It's more romantic to say "film." It
makes the story feel that much more long ago in a place far away.

I relished describing what it was like inside the little white church,
how the Bibles were still left open in the pews and how cold the
altar was. I built up the suspense with imaginings of Piney Grove. I
felt my dialect slowing down; I felt a florid drawl creeping in.

But I still wanted the lasting image to be true: what I discovered on
the hood of Molly's car beneath the warped lights of the gas station.
I remember my ears ringing, louder this time, much louder. I
remember the hunter-green paint of Molly's Mazda. Sprawled there
on the hood was a forest of little handprints in bright orange dust,
as if the hands of countless children had been pressed there, sticky
with thick pollen dust. The spring air is always so heavy with it.

That summer, I was headed to Mexico for a language immersion
program. To free up memory card space in my still-new digital
camera, I deleted every single photo from Piney Grove AME Zion
Church save one: a close-up of a starkly orange handprint.

Only a single print of the photo survives today. I keep it hanging
above my writing desk to try to keep the colors right in my
head, always. The dust really was so orange, something like rust,
something like pollen, something like the red dirt of home.

In the photo, you can see the hand that made the print was
furled into something like a fist. The handprint is smudged as if
the movement to make it had been rushed and spontaneous, like
banging on the hood of a stranger's car parked where it shouldn't
have been. I can see the white-hot glare of the fluorescent lights

against the sheen of the car. I can make out, too, the reflection of my hands trying to hold the camera steady.

Hovering over my shoulder is the wispy face of a little girl with braids in her hair, her mouth open in a laugh or a scream.

I am writing to you with the smell of fresh flowers dying, a bunch of lavender picked on a Sunday morning, bound with a white ribbon, hanging from a white wall. I am doing OK.

My partner and I seek out expansive green spaces. He drives just under five miles, pays for parking, and we take long, near-silent walks hand in hand for hours. I have asked my partner to stop kissing my hand, a habit I love, but it feels too dangerous.

These walks soften the edges of the homesickness I am waiting to be named. I feel I would give anything to walk the red dirt of home. I feel I would give anything. I know you know I mean it when I say it is this sickness that is my slow dying. I know you know that the home I am sick for was never, home was never. And, so, home is forever, too. What I mean is, once I wrote a poem for my father, who has only ever read stilted and broken birthday cards from me, some years reading 셍일 and 사랑해, others reading 생일 and 사랑헤:

sad man,

I found while spring cleaning, a picture
I took of a banana you wrote
on, ballpoint
pen on peel, "only
banana" and I remember thinking

I don't know what this means, but
this is how I want to remember you

thank you, sad man, for all the sandwiches
you've ever made me, no one else
will place so many things between
bread for my sake

and I want to tell my father, I wrote this for you when I was
eighteen? Nineteen? In the years before that, too young as you well
know, I was always writing for you and mother as if I were preparing
for death (yours, hers, or mine). Please know I am so proud of you.
Please know I love you so much.

These days, my mother sometimes asks me if there's anything going
on I'm not telling her. Specifically, she asks if I feel I can't tell her
things because she's always coming to me with her difficulties. In
these moments, my initial response is anger, that bitter sour tart
spark when I want to spit at my mother, Why didn't you ask me
when I was younger? Why didn't you consider making this space for
me when I was a child? I long and I long, still, to tattle to my mother
what's been done to me.

These days, when the fear that my parents will die before I see them
again is too great, I reread the letter my father wrote me, once, and
tell myself that not everything has to be said. Not everything has
to be written or spoken. It is possible and it is OK for things to be
unsaid. But I also think about how it took a man's writing, a man's
direction, the vision of men to move my father to open up to me, and
it again takes me back to unknowable fruit, and I am unspeakably,
heartbrokenly jealous at the thought that nothing I write may ever

move my father in this way, that he has felt what he felt and opened as he did, then, and now that moment already exists, it already is.

Each impossible day, I am waiting for the name built into the ground by the writers who came before me and twice-blessed by the writers who will come some unknowable time after I am dead. The writers after that will come into that place knowing it is ours. The writers after that will unbind the ropes and let down the bells that mark the furthermost boundaries. I hold hope I might live to read some of these words to come.

This hope is why and how I really fucking love my job, my relentless job. I read and I read, even when I can't write I have to keep reading, but sometimes I read a daughter's story about a mother who is becoming a shadow and think, How is it that you are my student? My student's story is slow green and fresh dying. I think about how my student will write five, ten years from now, and I hear the promise, I hear the unbound bells laid to rest upon the dark earth. Theresa 학경 Cha writes, "Earth is dark. Darker."

Theresa 학경 Cha writes:

> Lift me up mom to the window the child looking above too high above her view the glass between some image a blur now darks and greys mere shadows lingering above her vision her head tilted back as far as it can go.

Theresa 학경 Cha writes:

> Lift me to the window to the picture image unleash the ropes tied to weights of stones first the ropes then its scraping on wood to break stillness as the bells fall peal follow the sound

of ropes holding weight scraping on wood to break stillness
bells fall a peal to the sky.

I teach my students not to do this, a quote after a quote after a
quote. Where is the analysis, I task them. Where are you in relation
to the text?

Theresa 학경 Cha writes and she writes. She shows us how language
can protect by keeping out as much as letting in. Her protection is
invitation. Her invitation is protection. There she is in all the red
above and all the blue below, which is and is not the home I am
missing in a killing way, in a dying way. I have always been reading
my way home.

This morning, I passed my probation. I thought of you when I
received an official letter, jumbling my Korean name, notifying
me that I am now fully confirmed in post, a full-time lecturer on
a permanent contract, difficult to fire. I thought of my audacity to
write to you, that first time, as if I am a participant in change for
the better.

I asked for a revised copy, and now the letter mostly uses my name
correctly, but closes with:

> The Panel wish to congratulate you on the basis of your con-
> tributions to the Department of XXX.

I believe confirmation of post is something like tenure in America,
but way worse. Not just because in America I could call myself
professor. Still, it is a letter I would have liked to show my parents,
but the misuse of our names is always stinging and it will be my
father who will ask me:

XXX 는 무슨뜻?

But it will be my mother who is more loudly hurt by the thought that anyone could be so careless with something so important to me, to us.

Our first year or so in America, we lived in an apartment complex popular with immigrant families. The one next door to us had just moved from Germany, months after us. The parents spoke a little English, but their son, Amos, spoke none. Not even the word "apple," which I had known how to say and spell when I arrived. Amos hardly spoke, period, I only ever heard him whisper in German to his parents, but we were both seven or eight years old and our parents wanted us to be friends.

One day, somehow, my dad became convinced that Amos's father had been trying to tell him about a waterfall in South Carolina. We can fish there, my father said. And we can play in the water, like we used to. My dad was so excited in his gentle way. I hadn't seen my dad so excited in America before. I could remember much better then, I hope, swimming after him in rivers and lakes, surrounded by family and friends who looked like us and talked like us. I remember dozing against my father's back as he carried me across a favorite fishing spot, heading back to our campsite for the night. I don't think it occurred to either of us to be afraid of the deep and quiet dark. We were together, marveling at the infinite stars above us.

Throughout the week, my dad stayed up late studying a road map of South Carolina. My mother chose the morning we set out early, and although she wasn't sure about dad's plan, she'd spent the whole day before preparing a picnic for us to take.

This was before I learned to be nervous about my mother's cooking, before I told her I didn't want her to pack me any Korean food for school lunches, before an elementary school teacher came to stand by my seat in the cafeteria, sniffing the air around me as she asked, "Why do you smell so sour?"

We drove and we drove. We drove until we grew too tired of empty fields and stopped at an ancient-looking gas station, most of its small glass front covered with flag paraphernalia.

Go inside and ask for directions, my mom said, and paused before handing me a five-dollar bill. And buy something if you need to use the bathroom.

Where you from? The man behind the counter spoke slowly and had a soft, warm voice.

Korea, I knew to say. South.

An young hah say yo! he said.

Were you in the war? I knew to ask. And the man behind the counter was real pleased and talked for a long time.

Do you know where the waterfall is? I asked.

What waterfall?

Then the man turned to the window and pointed out to the empty field across the way. I noticed a tree at the center, tall but not too tall, with a thick trunk and sturdy-looking limbs, but without any leaves in this sunlit season. Good for climbing, I remember thinking.

"That there is a hanging tree. Where we used to hang—"

What did he say? my mother asked.

He asked me where I came from, I said.

Where's the change?

I spent it all, I said.

Why did you buy so much? You know we brought food from home. I was cooking all day yesterday. Do you want it to go to waste?

We never found a waterfall. The closest thing we found was a dam by some kind of factory or plant and we ate my mom's picnic there, in the car. The drive home was miserable, my mother nagging my father for this senseless trip and everything else, me eating too many snacks, all the snacks, and feeling something soupy curdling in my stomach.

The story doesn't end here.

That fall, Amos and I went trick-or-treating together, a first for us both. I was a witch and he was a scarecrow. Amos's hair was the exact color of the straw his mother had glued around his sleeves, his eyes as baby blue as the checks of his flannel shirt. Amos still didn't speak any English, at least not to me or to anyone I'd ever seen, but I remember thinking: He'll be just fine with his hair and his eyes, he'll be OK here.

At every door, I was the one to shout, Trick-or-treat, while Amos remained a step behind me, silent. But it was his costume the grown-ups cooed over; it was his hair the adults doling out the candy reached out to stroke. When our plastic pumpkins grew heavy, we trudged back home in silence. Amos's dad was waiting for us on the shared lawn and invited me in. We sat around their kitchen table and Amos's mom brought us juice. She asked me about school and how I liked being in America.

I miss my Korean friends, I said, looking at silent Amos.

Amo's father went to the kitchen and returned with the largest bag of pretzels I had ever seen in my young life. He tore into the bag and began to scoop handfuls of pretzels into my pumpkin.

Amos is so shy, his mother said. Like his father.

When I got home, I showed my mom my haul. What is that? she said. Why are there loose pretzels in your pumpkin? Who put them there? Why would someone do that? She kept asking why, growing more upset, picking out the pretzels as quickly as she could and gathering them into a dish.

Maybe it's normal in Germany, I said.

This is America, my mother said, pouring the pretzels into the trash. It was the first time in my life I had ever seen my mother throw unspoiled food away, my mother who ingrained in me so deep that rice is grown through blood, sweat, and tears of hard labor that to this day, eating the last bit of white, white rice from the belly of a porcelain bowl, I think I taste traces of minerals and feel a quiet stirring of awe and gratitude. This is where the story ends, in that small space that remains vivid still, in which I was stunned, momentarily, by my mother's Americanness, so decided in doing something I thought I would never, ever see her do, and, in turn, my own Koreanness, held dearer to me.

I keep wanting to trace how I came to be here, one day, feeling so far away, in a position of power I could hold more firmly than hope. One day, I may move on from this tracing and find firmer footing in the love and joy of such an ugly exquisite sculpture made from desiccated squid. Desiccated squid hands, desiccated squid breasts, a skirt that is all desiccated legs, desiccated tentacles, one large painted eye, one red silk braid. Fi Jae Lee calls this piece *Everything that Ascends to Heaven Smells Rotten*, and it is the cover art for her mother's book.

My first year on the job, in an outpouring to a colleague I trust about the fear of getting fired during probation, the kind and gentle colleague said, Well, just try not to kill anyone. I found this very reassuring. I thought, Yes, I can do that.

Dear Manchester Chinatown, I thought of you on this day of confirmation and how, one day, in that lovely red-brick flat in your neighborhood, I answered my door to a police officer who was surveying residents in the area for their opinion of the police. I was so startled, and so, I was so nice. I was so polite. But the tension didn't ease from the officer's face until I found myself answering, Yes—yes, I am Catholic. I'm not. I mean, not really. My father was raised Catholic. His parents, who were so vicious to my mother, were Catholic. I don't know why I said I was. But the cop was so surprised and spoke so warmly to me then, the air between us easier, and somewhere out there, there might exist, still, some police record of me as a Catholic resident of your neighborhood.

I say they were vicious, my father's parents, but they also gifted me a cross engraved with 김수진 and KOREA on the eve of my immigration. My mother says it was made from melting down their wedding bands, a sign that in spite of how they treated her, they did care for me, but my mother also makes up stories. There's a Korean expression for this, said often in anger or exasperation:

You're writing a novel.

What it means is, Stop lying. What it means is, Shut your mouth. Or, Tell the truth.

At a clinic in London, a year or two before the pandemic, when I was getting a birth control implant, the nurse and I discovered that we had both lived and studied in Manchester at around the same time, her for medicine and me for creative writing, though literature is what I told her. I still do this. I say, I teach literature. I suppose I'm writing a novel. It's a habit that comes from my own shame, guilt, and insecurity, just as much as from how I don't want to hear any more men informing me about the novel they've always been meaning to write or sending me a first chapter they wrote overnight. I don't want to hear about their research into geishas. I don't want to hear how nice they think Asian women are, what good wives Asian women make. I want to be left alone, as much as I want to go home.

The nurse from Manchester asked me if I'd been in Fallowfield, too, and I said no, I lived in Chinatown.

She laughed and I tensed. But then she said, "You had money."

And I eased and laughed and said I was very lucky.

She cut into my arm. She said, "You had money." She slipped something inside me, a small little thing I couldn't bear to look at because I didn't want to see her small and precise blade. I feel faint when I see blades. I couldn't bear looking then and I couldn't bear looking later, at some point, when that small little thing was taken out of me for the torrential bleeding it caused and, too, the sense of depression, functional yet pervasive.

Both things were true. In your neighborhood, I was very lucky and I had money. I had a white British American man to take with me to viewings. I had a good landlord who really adored his flat and loved you and Manchester as a whole. It was clear he had a long history with the city, a wilder life before the one he was just starting to settle into with his girlfriend and child on the way.

We did not speak much over those years, my landlord and I, but I remember I emailed him when a man climbed up the scaffolding that had been up around the building for months, and broke into the flat above mine. The man had tried my window first, but found it locked. I heard the jiggling while I was feeding my secret cat. I didn't mention my secret cat in my email to my landlord, of course, or that I had felt paralyzed by an animal fear. I suppose I should have called the cops, but I'm still not sure what I would have said. Hello, I thought I heard my window jiggling, but I'm too scared to pull up the blinds. I'm too scared to look outside. Also, could you please not tell my landlord about my secret cat? Also, you may have me down as Catholic, but I'm afraid I've made a rather silly mistake. My landlord responded straightaway and told me he was glad I was OK and that he was sorry that we couldn't have guns like in America, where I could have "unloaded a nine-millimeter into the bastard." He also told me that if anyone breaks in, I should run outside the flat and double-lock the door behind me. I found this very reassuring, too.

On the rare, maybe two, in-person visits my landlord made during my four years there, both times he thanked me for being a great tenant and specifically for not running a meth lab from his flat. In turn, he kept my rent fixed for all that time and only asked for a modest rise when he'd had his second or third child. I couldn't afford it then, and the timing was right for me to move on. It's what happens sometimes: we leave homes we love that were never really ours, grateful that they kept us safe, grateful that the owners were good people we never had to speak about politics with.

In the last two years of my Ph.D., to be able to afford rent as it was, I worked as a receptionist at an upscale hair salon, and it was exactly what many institutional instructors of creative writing claim their workshop spaces are: a nonpolitical space. It meant I missed a lot of extracurricular events at the university, including readings by visiting authors. But I was stunned when an author and professor whose event I had missed turned out to be a regular of the salon, routinely visiting for their signature £150 haircut. Could that be me one day? What shall we name this other fear, quiet and easily held, non-animal and, so, privileged, functional, and pervasive?

Dear Manchester Chinatown, my first letter to you was what was accepted by my institution as my formal research output, submitted to REF. I gather that I will not receive many stars, but however few must suffice. More shameful than the possibility of having too few stars to my name is the sense of the piece feeling grossly entitled in trying to speak to everyone who must cope with the perpetual and often profound sense of loss for what could have been in a life more restful: a community, a family, a self. In this sense, I wonder if I have rounded out too much, crafted too much for a sense of hope. Sometimes I actually do feel nauseated with worry about how gross my work might be, but lately I think about a trusted mentor who, when I used the word "gross" really bitterly to describe something I distinctly knew was so, so gross, my unfaltering friend agreed and said in her calm, soothing way, "Yes, very soupy." And when I think about that word in her voice, I feel OK. I feel OK if I write soup sometimes.

About a year after my first letter to you, I asked my first agent to release me from our contract. It was very painful to admit that my first novel was soup. It was very painful to admit that I could not finish any novel until I wrote this, this other book, with my first letter to you, not exactly at the center, but toward it.

My first agent did not want this, this other book, and that's just what happens sometimes: good people with good intentions who cannot come to rest on the matter of a book or two. It was very painful to let go of someone I admire very much who showed me so much good faith for years, years, someone who introduced me to an editor whose reader's reports still set the standard I hold myself to for feedbacking student work. I think of the editor and my first agent as I am kind on the job. I think of the editor and my first agent as I am rigorous.

As I prepare to enter the fourth year of my first permanent lectureship, theoretically as secure as I can be in my post, I feel just as unsettled as I ever was, albeit in unimaginably different ways. I don't know what to say to students who ask me how to write in these times, but this is what worked for me: Accept that you are second-rate. Be soup? Be sick? Be sick a lot. Cry all the time. But, also, be furious. Hold your fury close. Forgive nothing. Maybe some things. Stay bitter, though. And be sure to stay other words, too. You are sour. You are tart. Be delicious without shame. Toni Morrison said of those who would follow in the work of Black women writers, "They will write infinitely better than I do. They will write all sorts of things that no one writer can ever touch. They will be stronger, and they will be delicious to read." You are a reader. You are a writer. No one can grant or deny you stars. The real stars are in the sky all around you at all times, at all times dead and dying. Know these things well but also not really believe the words. Write until you find something that can only be surmised as balance while knowing that this is not the right word. Write new words if you need to and stare down anyone who tries to tell you to put them in italics or include a glossary because this is how things are done. Ask why. Ask why without a question mark at the end. Say all the silent parts out loud. Thrive in discomfort.

But, also: Ask for help. Trust deeply in the kindness of writers and readers who help you.

But, also: Keep questioning how much of the work we do relies on what we name to be trust. Recognize there are many animal-things we so name. Delicious things. Gently-gently. Lovingly. What kills.

Survive. Cope. Get through. Think about getting out. Stay in that space of possibility. Get out if you really need to. Leave as safely and as strongly as possible.

I know even less what to say to students who are being evicted from their homes, losing jobs, losing disability support, losing mental health support, losing family, losing loved ones. So many of my students have never been able to afford living in London in the first place, and now I can only imagine how the days may feel like a recurring nightmare. I am sorry. I will keep trying to imagine, as do the writers whose books I hold close and stack together and hold close and stack together until I am not my job. 언니라고 불러도 될까요? 잘 부탁드립니다.

I will keep trying to stay healthy and happy enough to keep trying.

I have daydreams of being able to fund a scholarship for first-generation immigrants to pursue higher education, abroad should they wish, as I did. I have daydreams that some will choose to go home. I have daydreams of naming such a scholarship after my mother, after my father. My mother first, so that I can take her by the hand and say, Look, what you did for me, what you did for your sisters, I will do for others. I will do so without grinding down my bones as hard as yours. I will do so comfortably. I realize I am already settling into a life of such comfort to dream in this way.

If my book does well, I could negotiate with that power. I could teach less. I could write more. And now I have, not one, but two dream agents: an agent in London, an agent in New York. They are agents I would not have had access to without my job. In our first conversation, my London agent said, so surely, "I mean, you know when something is finished." And I found that I could really hear her. I found that I did know, or, at least, I could see how I might get there. And I found this startling.

I should confess that I did not pick the lavender myself. It was picked for me, and I, in turn, picked up the bundle at a drive-through, socially-distanced farm shop where the purveyors had rubber-banded a card-reader to the end of a fence post that they held out to the driver's-side window.

I paid London prices for fresh lavender. I held the lavender with both hands and it felt so luxurious. Just as I was about to dip my head into the bouquet, I noticed some kind of large insect attached to one of the flowers. I shrank away and closed my eyes and asked my partner to pick it off gently-gently.

When my partner passed the lavender back to me, I saw half of the insect still attached, filaments of something silken and fibrous furling out of the broken shell, some cocoon or chrysalis or whatever that stage is, before, before.

"You killed it," I said, too sad for such a small death.

"Circle of life and all that," my partner said, too easily. It made us laugh, the absurdity of what he said, how he said it, as if any of this, all of this all around us, our gesturing wildly with both hands all around us, is easy. We talked about *The Lion King* and I even sang some of the song and we laughed most of the way home because my partner didn't mean what he said. This small death pained him just as much as me, possibly more, as he was directly responsible.

I can see myself continuing to ease into a life where I have maybe too much room to feel small deaths, too much room to make them poignant for myself, too much room where I risk losing sight of the immediacy and urgency of harder, harsher truths. I worry about growing soft and sheltered, which I know, or I used to know, better the further back I reach, I know this kind of safety lends itself so easily to cruelty. Going forward, I can see how easy it would be to tell myself that it won't happen to me.

I won't stop worrying that my writing will grow confident in a way that is careless and I won't stop worrying that one day no one will be around to edit me because I will stop listening.

There will never come a day when I look back on the words I wrote here, for this other book that is not a novel, while trying to survive a new job and an unprecedented global pandemic—and feel shame for so exposing my own desperation.

I will open this other book with the only Korean poem I have ever written. The Korean used is likely broken and outdated—but it is my own. The poem came to me as fully formed as it could be (considering my mutated Korean), in the span of time it took for me to walk from my childhood bedroom to the kitchen of my family home. In the poem, I am home alone with my father, observing him doing dishes at the sink, while my mother is away in Korea visiting her dying sister. The poem makes no direct mention of my mother coping with her sister dying, noting only my mother's absence. There is some sense that my mother might be dead. My mother and her sister were the closest in age of their siblings, and my mother tells me they looked very much alike in their youth with their snow-white, full-moon faces. They are present, my mother and her sister (my aunt I hardly remember as she is dying), in the poem's closing focus on a rice bowl my father holds, gleaming like a pearl.

I translated the poem into a monologue from my grieving mother. When I asked my partner to read it over, he made that *oof* sound he makes when he reads my work before very sweetly expressing his concern for my mother. Would she be upset by this airing of our dirty laundry? I got what I've been told is prickly and I told him, This isn't my actual mother actually speaking, my mother doesn't speak like this, my mother doesn't speak English. I got what I've been told is sharp, but I know you know that the voice I am writing is not my mother's. Through this imagined, other voice of my mother, I found room to speak to things unsaid between me, my mother, and my father. I know you know that when I say "unsaid," I mean the saying and the not and the taking back, too. In the monologue, instead of speaking directly of her sister's death, the character of my mother poses questions around both the possibility and certainty of her own death and how my father and I would survive. The poem and the monologue are extensions of one another, sisters in shared in-between spaces. I know you know that if you have only ever lived with one country to call home, I can't explain that kind of dark to you, out where nothing lasts, not even God's house.

In the months after my confirmation of post, my department will add a new section to the form we are tasked to fill out in advance of research productivity meetings. It doesn't happen yet, not in the space of time in which this letter to you opens, the space in which I am writing to you on the bright morning of my confirmation with birdsong at my window, the confirmation I worked so hard for that it becomes easy to think words are more reassuring than they are not. But this is what writing can do. Writing can reassure and writing can upset, writing can disrupt. Writing can control time at will and I can evoke the aftermath of a book before the book is finished.

The first UK publication of a collection of Audre Lorde's essential works is entitled *Your Silence Will Not Protect You* (2017). In "Uses of Anger," Lorde quotes from her poem "For Each of You":

everything can be used
except what is wasteful
(you will need
to remember this when you are accused of destruction.)

A new section on my department's mandatory research productivity form reads:

You may need to submit your research project to your Department Research Ethics Office for ethical review if you answer yes to the following questions:

- Does your project pose any risk to the welfare or interests of any human participant, group or their data? y/n
- Are you putting your own welfare or interests at risk by carrying out the research activity? y/n
- Is the welfare of any animal at risk? y/n
- Does your project risk causing damage or change to cultural heritage? y/n
- Does your project risk causing changes to the natural environment? y/n
- Does your project risk compromising the reputation of individuals, the department, the College, the discipline or academia? y/n
- Does your project risk compromising the welfare and interests of the wider college community? y/n

It may be helpful to consider these questions from different perspectives, for example:

- Could you happily justify your activity to your manager or a colleague or friend?
- What would your actions look like if publicised in the media?
- What could go wrong as a result of your activity for you, your colleagues (staff and students), other stakeholders or the wider College/discipline/community?
- Is it your decision to make?

In this time to come, roles and titles will change. The department will make gestures toward transparent workloads. I will stare and stare at a spreadsheet accounting for the teaching hours and student numbers of the heavenly line boats who endlessly offered the advice to just write for two to four hours every day—and if I can't do that, well, well.

I will decide to leave, and I will decide to stay. I will encounter a
senior colleague on my last day on the job, this particular job that
was once a dream, and their parting words to me will be to say that
I won't get far in my new department, my new school, biting the
hand that feeds me.

In this time to come, I will be on the phone with my mother about
a customer stealing the bells off our store door, the cloisonné bells
she brought back from Korea, from the Buddhist temple where her
mother, my grandmother, had her 사십구재. I will be trying to
listen without becoming too upset, distracting myself by finishing
what I was working on just before she called—y/n, y/n, y/n, y/n,
y/n, y/n. Eventually, my mother will say, It's not a big deal. The
bells are gone, but no one was hurt. No one was hurt. And we will
close out the phone call by taking turns to say, 몸조심, 또 몸조심
and get home before dark. Instead of reminding my mother that I
teach evening classes, I will ride the twist of anxiety and give in to
the urge to scold her. And I will not fully face the way I sound too
sharp, too angry with my mother as I tell her: It's more dangerous
for you now. It's more dangerous for you than for me. You have seen
the news. You have seen the images. Your sisters, they used to call
you 독한년, they used to say I got it from you, but you aren't that
anymore, are you? I know, these days, you would stand so small and
still and shaking for anyone who approaches you, scared most of all
about the likelihood of not understanding what they might say to
you, but never expecting a fist—or worse.

But, for now, on this bright morning, I am confirmed in post. Dear
Manchester Chinatown, I am, I have been confirmed, and I'm
thinking of you today and I wanted to write to you to close this
book, with a small death and a small life, y/n, and to tell you that

when we moved to America, my mother forbade me from writing in my journal in Korean. She said it was for our own good.

I can't say for sure why my mother made the choices she did. I don't know what it was like for her to land in Hawaii, convinced she could ease into the life of an immigrant by starting it with a vacation. I don't know what it was like for her to walk to her first American food stall to ask for a bag of chips. She asked for a snack, what they were called in Korea back then. Snack, please, she said, and the man behind the counter scowled. WHAT? he said. Snack, please, my mother said more slowly. NO, he said, visibly repulsed, squaring his shoulders. NO, NO SNAKE. NO SNAKE! I DON'T SELL SNAKE. I can't say for sure how my mother could laugh about it then and laugh about it now. When she tells the story again, when she still has to pause to reach for the word "chips," I expel something like a laugh mostly through my nose. I smile with my lips tight to try to hold back what is slithering up my throat. I feel exhausted.

I don't want to say any more than that about that, but one day, before my mother bought me a puppy she came to love as close as she could to the son she almost had, before our beloved dog died at the age of nineteen and we buried him in our backyard covering his small grave with stones we brought down from the mountains, before my mother began to say out loud, looking up at the sky, and I know that's where she's looking, even when we are on the phone and I can only hear her voice on the line—이제 정 주는개 너무 무섭다, 무서워—I was nine or ten and practicing piano while my mother was doing dishes in the kitchen—and a bird flew in through some open window, somewhere.

I saw the bird first and called for my mother. She didn't believe me at first. What do you mean? she said. A bird, I said, there's a bird in the house. She didn't believe me until she saw it, too. Then she was the one to ask me, What should we do?

Just after my Ph.D., just as I was starting the job hunt, miserable and unwell and trying to decide whether marriage was right for me, my partner and I went to see a couples therapist. How hard could it have been to find a first-generation, female-identifying therapist of color in London? Why didn't I press for it? I remember the therapist we did see interjecting to say that he was struck by the way I said I grew up navigating life for my parents. He took time to savor the word "navigating." I could feel that he was saying it with great sensitivity and some sense of admiration, but I remember feeling exasperated and, too, exhausted, as I so often am, exhausted, at the thought that we weren't going to get very far if he was going to marvel at my aptitude for language, or how different my life was from most people's, i.e., from his.

I told my mom that we needed to catch it, the bird. What else could we do? We couldn't just leave a bird in the house. We couldn't just wait for dad to come home. With his rough, clumsy hands, my father would surely snap its neck. We needed some sort of netting, a shawl, a sheet, something. My mother ran upstairs and ran back down holding a lace tablecloth. I recognized it as something she'd had since she was a young woman in Korea, younger than the age I am now. I recognized it as something delicate, and precious to her. As well, I understood, innately, why my mother had reached for this in something like panic, net-like and so light, exactly as I had described, perfect for our attempt to capture the bird but, also, and more importantly: My mother didn't want the bird to get hurt. She couldn't bear the bird getting hurt.

We ran lightly through the house, my mother and I, leaping with the lace held between us. Somehow, in spite of our high ceilings and our (slightly below) average heights, we caught the bird in the lace. We held the tablecloth like a candy wrapper between us, bunching the lace in our hands by the ends, watching the desperate little flutter at the center until the bird settled down with muted shock.

We hurried, gently-gently, outside, onto our back porch. We unwound the lace slowly. For no more than two heartbeats, the bird was perfectly still, balancing atop the lace and taking turns to study our faces, my mother's and mine, and we could see then just how small and perfect it was, the little house sparrow we had caught.

Then it flew. We watched until it flew out of sight, as if it had never interrupted our day at all. We stood on the patio for some time after that, prolonging the moment with our heads, not turned to the sky, but bent close together, checking the lace. We examined the lace, again and again, just as slowly, just as carefully each time. I thought I remembered the way the lace had sat on a low table in the center of our apartment in the center of Seoul, how it had brushed my knees as I stretched my legs out beneath the table and touched my toes to my father's, to my mother's. The sun was so bright that my mother and I had to squint to make out the finer points of the working. We worked our hands through and through the lace and found it to be intact.

김수진 올림
June 30, 2021

X X X

Ahluwalia, Aman, "Why Won't Birkbeck Deal with Its Problem of Racist Academic Staff?," *gal-dem* (November 13, 2019), https://gal-dem.com/why-wont-birkbeck-deal-with-its-problem-of-racist-academic-staff/.

Ahmed, Sara, "Complaint and Survival," *feministkilljoys* (March 23, 2020), https://feministkilljoys.com/2020/03/23/complaint-and-survival/.

배수아, <뱀과 물> 문학동네, 2017.

Baldwin, James, *Go Tell It on the Mountain* (Knopf, 2013).

봉준호, <기생충> CJ 엔터테인먼트, 2019.

Brodber, Erna, *Louisiana: A Novel* (New Beacon, 1994).

Cha, Theresa Hak Kyung, *Dictee* (University of California Press, 2001).

Chan, Mary Jean, *Flèche* (Faber, 2019).

Chee, Alexander, "How to Unlearn Everything: When It Comes to Writing the 'Other,' What Questions Are We Not Asking?," *Vulture* (October 30, 2019), https://www.vulture.com/2019/10/author-alexander-chee-on-his-advice-to-writers.html.

Chesnutt, Charles W., *The Conjure Woman and Other Conjure Tales* (Duke University Press, 1993).

Chingonyi, Kayo, *A Blood Condition* (Chatto, 2021).

Choi, Don Mee, *Hardly War* (Wave, 2016).

Choi, Don Mee, *DMZ Colony* (Wave, 2020).

Chu, Andrea Long, "I Worked with Avital Ronell. I believe Her Accuser," *Chronicle of Higher Education* (August 30, 2018), https://www.chronicle.com/article/i-worked-with-avital-ronell-i-believe-her-accuser/.

Collins, Wilkie, *The Woman in White* (1860), Project Gutenberg, posted September 13, 2008, http://www.gutenberg.org/files/583/583-h/583-h.htm.

Daniels, Kate, "Old Masters: Review of *Thieves of Paradise* by Yusef Komunyakaa," *Southern Review* 35.3 (Summer 1999), 621–634.

Derricotte, Toi, "The Tension Between Memory and Forgetting in the Poetry of Yusef Komunyakaa," *Kenyon Review* 15, no. 4 (Autumn 1993), 217–222.

Dweck, Anthony C., "The folklore of *Narcissus*," *Narcissus and Daffodil: The Genus Narcissus*, ed. by Gordon R. Hanks (Taylor & Francis, 2002), 19–29.

Eddo-Lodge, Reni, *Why I'm No Longer Talking to White People About Race* (Bloomsbury, 2018).

Eng, David L., and Shinhee Han, *Racial Melancholia, Racial Dissociation: On the Social and Psychic Lives of Asian Americans* (Duke University Press, 2019).

Fulton, Sybrina, *Rest in Power: The Enduring Life of Trayvon Martin* (Spiegel & Grau, 2017).

<한 번 다녀왔습니다>, KBS2, 2020.

hooks, bell, "Representing Whiteness in the Black Imagination," in *Displacing Whiteness: Essays in Social and Cultural Criticism* (Duke University Press, 1999), 165–179.

Hunter-Gault, Charlayne, "PBS NewsHour: Toni Morrison on Beloved, 1987 Interview," posted August 6, 2019, https://youtu.be/pLQ6ipVRfrE.

Jones, Bessie, *Get in Union* (Odyssey Productions, 2020).

Kenan, Randall, *Let the Dead Bury Their Dead* (Abacus, 1994).

Kim, Hyesoon, *I'm OK, I'm PIG!* (Bloodaxe, 2014).

Komunyakaa, Yusef, *Neon Vernacular* (Wesleyan University Press, 1993).

Lead Belly, *Lead Belly's Last Sessions* (Smithsonian Folkways Recordings, 1994).

Lorde, Audre, *Your Silence Will Not Protect You* (Silver Press, 2017).

Mathis, Johnny, *Song Sung Blue* (Jon Mat Records, 2016).

Michel, Lincoln, "Lush Rot," *Guernica* (March 17, 2014), https://www.guernicamag.com/lincoln-michel-lush-rot/.

Milbank, Alison, "Victorian Gothic in English Novels and Stories, 1830–1880," *The Cambridge Companion to Gothic Fiction*, ed. by Jerrold E. Hogle (Cambridge University Press, 2002), 145–166.

Mills, Jerry Leath, "Equine Gothic: The Dead Mule as Generic Signifier in Southern Literature of the Twentieth Century," *The Southern Literary Journal* 29, no. 1 (Fall 1996), 2–17.

Mississippi John Hurt, *Complete Studio Recordings* (Vanguard Records, 2006).

Morrison, Toni, *Mouth Full of Blood* (Chatto & Windus, 2019).

나홍진, <곡성> 사이드미러, 2016.

Page, Kezia, " 'Two Places Can Make Children': Erna Brodber's *Louisiana*," *Journal of West Indian Literature* 13, no. 5 (April 2005), 57–79.

Park, Josephine Nock-Hee, " 'What of the Partition': Dictée's Boundaries and the American Epic," *Contemporary Literature* 46, no. 2 (Summer 2005), 213–242.

Park, Si-soo, "Unlikely Fan of Korean Drama in US," *Korea Times* (February 2, 2014), http://www.koreatimes.co.kr/www/news/culture/2014/02/386_151384.html.

Pearson, Jane and Hew D. V. Prendergast, "Daemonorops, Dracaena and Other Dragon's Blood," *Economic Botany* 55, no. 4 (October–December 2001), 474–477.

Poe, Edgar Allen, "The Philosophy of Composition," *Essays and Reviews* (Library of America, 1984), 13–25.

Rankine, Claudia, *Citizen: An American Lyric* (Penguin, 2015).

Reinhardt, Uwe E., "Introductory Korean Drama," *OpenScholar@Princeton* (2014), https://scholar.princeton.edu/reinhardt/publications-0.

Ross, Janell, "How Black Lives Matter Moved from a Hashtag to a Real Life Political Force," *The Washington Post* (August 19, 2015), https://www.washingtonpost.com/news/the-fix/wp/2015/08/19/how-black-lives-matter-moved-from-a-hashtag-to-a-real-political-force/.

Salas, Angela M., "Race, Human Empathy, and Negative Capability: The Poetry of Yusef Komunyakaa," *College Literature* (Fall 2003), 32–53.

Sister Gertrude Morgan, *Let's Make A Record* (Ropeadope, 2004).

<심야괴담회>, MBC, 2021.

Stephens, Vincent, "Shaking the Closet: Analyzing Johnny Mathis's Sexual Elusiveness, 1956–82," *Popular Music and Society* 33, no. 5 (December 2010), 597–623.

Taylor, Leila, *Darkly: Black History and America's Gothic Soul* (Repeater Books, 2019).

Trethewey, Natasha D., "On Close Reading: Yusef Komunyakaa's 'White Lady,'" *Callaloo* 28, no. 3 (Summer 2005), 775–777.

Turner, Daniel Cross, "Dying Objects/Living Things: The Thingness of Poetry in Yusef Komunyakaa's Talking Dirty to the Gods," *Mosaic* 45, no. 1 (March 2012), 137–154.

"Violent History: Attacks on Black Churches," *The New York Times* (June 18, 2015), http://www.nytimes.com/interactive/2015/06/18/us/19blackchurch.html.

Warwick, Alexandra, "Gothic, 1820–1880," *Terror and Wonder: The Gothic Imagination*, ed. by Dale Townshend (British Library, 2014), 94–121.

Watkins, Gloria, "Where the Sick Lie," *Gumbo* 1 (1977), 9.

Yaeger, Patricia, "Ghosts and Shattered Bodies, or What Does it Mean to Still Be Haunted by Southern Literature?," *Southern Central Review* 22, no. 1 (Spring 2005), 87–108.

Yi, Tian, "Body Language," *CRAFT* (October 2, 2020), https://www.craftliterary.com/2020/10/02/body-language-tian-yi/.

Yronwode, Catherine, *Hoodoo Herb and Root Magic: A Materia Magica of African-American Conjure and Traditional Formulary Giving the Spiritual Uses of Natural Herbs, Roots, Minerals, and Zoological Curios* (Lucky Mojo Curio, 2002).

TO MY MOTHER TO MY FATHER
what an honor to be your daughter

Theresa Hak Kyung Cha's MAH-UHM is transcribed in 한글 in the epigraph. I wanted to open the text with her words and our 마음. I am grateful to the Berkeley Art Museum and Pacific Film Archive for giving me this space. Don Mee Choi's perspective on South Korea as a neocolony has been critical to shaping how I think, translate, and write. I am grateful for our email exchange that led to moments of refining I could not have achieved on my own. I am grateful, as well, to Wave Books for the generous permission to quote from Choi's works. Rama Lee created my author photo. Ingsu Liu designed my cover. I am grateful for your art, your care. In addition to the creators whose works I cite, I am indebted beyond words to Laura Joyce, Kathryn Pallant, Alys Conran, Anna Hartnell, Katherine Angel, Jude Bryan, KJ Orr, Malachi McIntosh, & Alba Ziegler-Bailey; M. Forajter at *Tarpaulin Sky Magazine* for homing "Dear Manchester Chinatown," with special thanks to Mary Jean Chan who read early drafts with generosity & grace; *Wasafiri*, especially my reader in 인천 for championing <정>; *Oxford American*, especially Hannah Saulters, Perrin Smith, & Danielle A. Jackson for pushing "한녀 [WOAMN, WHITE]" into something else; Nicole Hur at *The Hanok Review* for housing "WE ARE MOVING TO AMERICA"; Specimen Press for making me feel like a real poet & translator for a spell; Jill Bialosky, Drew Elizabeth Weitman, Dave Cole, & the team at Norton; Jacqueline Ko & Emma Smith for being dream agents; my students & colleagues for my dream job, with special thanks to Tatum Anderson, Katie Willis, Marisa Henderson, Asli Jensen, Akeela Bhattay, & Tian Yi; students & colleagues everywhere for doing the best we can. Thank you.

Danny, for your regular contributions to the Prof. W. & Mr. D. Kim Medical Fund. Thank you for taking Trouble on one of his last walks with me. He hated it. He hated leaving home, even for a short walk in the neighborhood; he couldn't bear not being able to see our house. I think often about this deep, likely neurotic sense of duty both innate and instilled in him that he had to be home, stay home. Dad said that on his last night, Trouble led him on a long walk through our house. They paused by the back door for some time, staring out at our yard. The birds, the squirrels, and the rabbits had stopped fearing Trouble, and he no longer gave them chase. With his bad hips and dad's bad knee, they took their time, dad switching off the lights and checking the doors along the way as Trouble nosed around the faded patterns of our mother's rugs, never quite the same after all the times he peed on them. Trouble sat for a while by my piano, in the exact spot where he used to listen while I practiced. They even went to my room, something Trouble never did when I wasn't home. That night, Trouble stood by my bedroom door until dad opened it for him. He stepped just beyond the threshold and stood so still in the dark for a long, long time, until dad told him it was time for bed. Then, Trouble went to bed. He slept as he always did after I left home, nestled between the heads of our mother & our father. 우리 쭐쭐이. My beautiful genius multilingual Trouble, when he met you, he loved you instantly. My parents and I had never seen him so adore an outside human before. We think he knew before any of us that you were meant to be my home. I remember Trouble curled up in your lap, and I better understand how love can be.